U.S. Department
of Transportation

Federal Railroad
Administration

# Understanding Driver Behavior at Grade Crossings through Signal Detection Theory

Office of Research
and Development
Washington DC 20590

## Human Factors in Railroad Operations

DOT/FRA/ORD-13-01

Final Report
January 2013

This document is available to the public through the National Technical Information Service, Springfield, VA 22161. This document is also available on the FRA Web site at www.fra.gov.

| 2. AGENCY USE ONLY (*LEAVE BLANK*) | 3. REPORT DATE<br>January 2013 | 3. REPORT TYPE AND DATES COVERED<br>Final Report | |
|---|---|---|---|
| 4. TITLE AND SUBTITLE<br>Understanding Driver Behavior at Grade Crossings through Signal Detection Theory | | | 5. FUNDING NUMBERS<br>RR04/XX |
| 6. AUTHOR(S)<br>Michelle Yeh, Thomas Raslear, and Jordan Multer | | | |
| 7. PERFORMING ORGANIZATION NAME(S) AND ADDRESS(ES)<br><br>U.S. Department of Transportation<br>Federal Railroad Administration<br>Office of Research and Development<br>Washington, DC 20590 | | | 8. PERFORMING ORGANIZATION<br><br>DOT-VNTSC-FRA |
| 9. SPONSORING/MONITORING AGENCY NAME(S) AND ADDRESS(ES)<br><br>U.S. Department of Transportation<br>Federal Railroad Administration<br>Office of Research and Development<br>Washington, DC 20590 | | | 10. SPONSORING/MONITORING AGENCY REPORT NUMBER<br><br>DOT/FRA/ORD-13/01 |
| 11. SUPPLEMENTARY NOTES<br>Program Manager: Thomas Raslear | | | |
| 12a. DISTRIBUTION/AVAILABILITY STATEMENT<br><br>This document is available to the public through the National Technical Information Service, Springfield, VA 22161, and on the FRA Web site at http://www.fra.dot.gov. | | | 12b. DISTRIBUTION CODE |

13. ABSTRACT (Maximum 200 words)

This report uses signal detection theory (SDT) to model motorists' decisionmaking strategies at grade crossings in order to understand the factors that influence such decisions and to establish a framework for evaluating the impact of proposed countermeasures. This report is intended to update and expand the original analysis conducted by Raslear (1996), which examined the effectiveness of grade crossing warning devices and determined whether their effectiveness was due to variations in the signal-to-noise ratio (sensitivity), bias to stop, or a combination of these two components of signal detection theory.

This report documents the results of four empirical and theoretical tests of the SDT model to understand how different warning devices and countermeasures influenced drivers' decisions at grade crossings in the 21 years from 1986 (as reported by Raslear) to 2007 (the most current year available when this effort began). In the first analysis, we compare accident data from 2007 with that from 1986 and describe the necessary adjustments to our assumptions in setting up the model. In the second analysis, we apply this revised framework to a more detailed historical analysis of driver decisionmaking at grade crossings. The third analysis describes our test of the robustness of the SDT model and our application of SDT to predict the effect of proposed countermeasures and safety factors. The fourth analysis was based on a theoretical model to test the predictive abilities of the SDT framework through performance by an ideal observer. While the previous analyses examine the empirical changes in sensitivity and bias over time and with changes in the grade crossing environment, the analysis of the ideal observer posits theoretical mechanisms for those changes and compares theoretical outcomes with actual outcomes.

| 14. SUBJECT TERMS<br>Highway-rail grade crossing, traffic control devices, signal detection theory, grade crossing safety, driver compliance, safety factors | | | 15. NUMBER OF PAGES<br>63 |
|---|---|---|---|
| | | | 16. PRICE CODE |
| 17. SECURITY CLASSIFICATION OF REPORT<br>Unclassified | 18. SECURITY CLASSIFICATION OF THIS PAGE<br>Unclassified | 19. SECURITY CLASSIFICATION OF ABSTRACT<br>Unclassified | 20. LIMITATION OF ABSTRACT |

# METRIC/ENGLISH CONVERSION FACTORS

| ENGLISH TO METRIC | METRIC TO ENGLISH |
|---|---|

## LENGTH (APPROXIMATE)

| ENGLISH TO METRIC | METRIC TO ENGLISH |
|---|---|
| 1 inch (in) = 2.5 centimeters (cm) | 1 millimeter (mm) = 0.04 inch (in) |
| 1 foot (ft) = 30 centimeters (cm) | 1 centimeter (cm) = 0.4 inch (in) |
| 1 yard (yd) = 0.9 meter (m) | 1 meter (m) = 3.3 feet (ft) |
| 1 mile (mi) = 1.6 kilometers (km) | 1 meter (m) = 1.1 yards (yd) |
|  | 1 kilometer (km) = 0.6 mile (mi) |

## AREA (APPROXIMATE)

| ENGLISH TO METRIC | METRIC TO ENGLISH |
|---|---|
| 1 square inch (sq in, $in^2$) = 6.5 square centimeters ($cm^2$) | 1 square centimeter ($cm^2$) = 0.16 square inch (sq in, $in^2$) |
| 1 square foot (sq ft, $ft^2$) = 0.09 square meter ($m^2$) | 1 square meter ($m^2$) = 1.2 square yards (sq yd, $yd^2$) |
| 1 square yard (sq yd, $yd^2$) = 0.8 square meter ($m^2$) | 1 square kilometer ($km^2$) = 0.4 square mile (sq mi, $mi^2$) |
| 1 square mile (sq mi, $mi^2$) = 2.6 square kilometers ($km^2$) | 10,000 square meters ($m^2$) = 1 hectare (ha) = 2.5 acres |
| 1 acre = 0.4 hectare (he) = 4,000 square meters ($m^2$) |  |

## MASS - WEIGHT (APPROXIMATE)

| ENGLISH TO METRIC | METRIC TO ENGLISH |
|---|---|
| 1 ounce (oz) = 28 grams (gm) | 1 gram (gm) = 0.036 ounce (oz) |
| 1 pound (lb) = 0.45 kilogram (kg) | 1 kilogram (kg) = 2.2 pounds (lb) |
| 1 short ton = 2,000 pounds (lb) = 0.9 tonne (t) | 1 tonne (t) = 1,000 kilograms (kg) = 1.1 short tons |

## VOLUME (APPROXIMATE)

| ENGLISH TO METRIC | METRIC TO ENGLISH |
|---|---|
| 1 teaspoon (tsp) = 5 milliliters (ml) | 1 milliliter (ml) = 0.03 fluid ounce (fl oz) |
| 1 tablespoon (tbsp) = 15 milliliters (ml) | 1 liter (l) = 2.1 pints (pt) |
| 1 fluid ounce (fl oz) = 30 milliliters (ml) | 1 liter (l) = 1.06 quarts (qt) |
| 1 cup (c) = 0.24 liter (l) | 1 liter (l) = 0.26 gallon (gal) |
| 1 pint (pt) = 0.47 liter (l) |  |
| 1 quart (qt) = 0.96 liter (l) |  |
| 1 gallon (gal) = 3.8 liters (l) |  |
| 1 cubic foot (cu ft, $ft^3$) = 0.03 cubic meter ($m^3$) | 1 cubic meter ($m^3$) = 36 cubic feet (cu ft, $ft^3$) |
| 1 cubic yard (cu yd, $yd^3$) = 0.76 cubic meter ($m^3$) | 1 cubic meter ($m^3$) = 1.3 cubic yards (cu yd, $yd^3$) |

## TEMPERATURE (EXACT)

| ENGLISH TO METRIC | METRIC TO ENGLISH |
|---|---|
| $[(x-32)(5/9)]$ °F = y °C | $[(9/5) y + 32]$ °C = x °F |

# QUICK INCH - CENTIMETER LENGTH CONVERSION

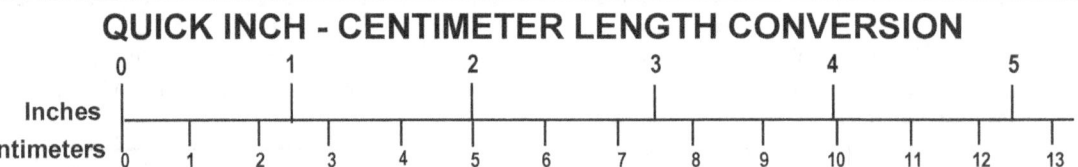

# QUICK FAHRENHEIT - CELSIUS TEMPERATURE CONVERSIO

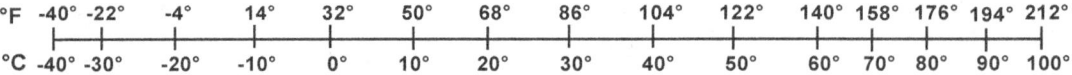

For more exact and or other conversion factors, see NIST Miscellaneous Publication 286, Units of Weights and Measures.

Price $2.50 SD Catalog No. C13 10286                      Updated 6/17/98

# ACKNOWLEDGEMENTS

This research was conducted with funding from the Federal Railroad Administration's (FRA) Office of Research and Development while the first author was a staff member at the John A. Volpe National Transportation Systems Center (the Volpe Center).

The views expressed herein are those of the authors and do not necessarily reflect the views of the Volpe Center, the Research and Innovative Technology Administration, or the U. S. Department of Transportation.

# Contents

# Illustrations

# Tables

## Executive Summary

From 1986 to 2007, collisions at highway-rail grade crossings decreased by over 50 percent while the aggregate number of trains per day at grade crossings increased by 125 percent, and the annual average daily traffic (AADT) at grade crossings increased by over 70 percent. What factors can explain this? Analysis shows that grade crossing warning devices—active warning devices, in particular—are the most important safety tool in preventing train-vehicle collisions because they increase the motorists' **willingness to stop** at the crossing. **Willingness to stop** is more important than improving motorists' ability to **detect the train**; even measures to improve train detection improve motorists' **willingness to stop**.

A widely accepted model of human behavior, Signal Detection Theory (SDT), was used to examine two key factors in grade crossing accidents: the ability of the motorist to **detect the presence of the train** and the motorist's **willingness to stop**. Motorists are able to **detect trains** based on the visibility and audibility of the train relative to its background, which may contain other objects and sounds. **Willingness to stop** is based on motorists' expectations ("I never see a train when I cross here") and motivation ("I'll be late for work if I have to wait for that train to pass and that will cost me an hour of pay"). SDT suggests that motorists make decisions either to stop or to proceed at grade crossings based on these two independent factors.

Since 1986 there has been a steady increase in the motorists' ability to detect trains and in their willingness to stop; this increase corresponds to the improvement in grade crossing safety noted above. During this time period, several grade crossing safety programs were implemented: improving commercial motor vehicle driver safety compliance with traffic safety laws through federal regulations, increasing locomotive conspicuity with alerting lights, increasing rail car conspicuity with retroreflective materials, increasing sight lines, and improving active warning device reliability. Thus, it was important to understand which safety programs led to this improvement in driver behavior and grade crossing safety. Ability to detect trains and willingness to stop was assessed for eight grade crossing warning device types and the five safety programs. Ability to detect trains increased by 3.2 percent as a result of the safety programs, but willingness to stop increased by 165 percent. Overall improvement in safety was due both to increases in ability to detect a train and willingness to stop, but willingness to stop was more important. A comparison of the effect of safety programs and grade crossing warning devices found that safety improved because of both grade crossing devices and safety factors, but grade crossing devices were nearly twice as effective.

The empirical findings from SDT were compared to the theoretical predictions of the SDT model for an ideal observer who represents *optimal* decisionmaking. The ideal observer can be used to develop a model of optimal performance and provide hypotheses about how driver behavior can be enhanced to prevent accidents. The ideal observer analysis showed trends similar to those for each of the safety factors in the empirical analysis. The ideal observer analysis confirms the empirical finding that willingness to stop offers a greater contribution to grade crossing safety outcomes than the driver's ability to detect the train. In fact, the analysis suggests that measures that improve train detection are effective to the extent that they also encourage drivers to stop.

The SDT model described here provides an analytical framework that illustrates the impact of other countermeasures for improving grade crossing safety. One of the key aspects of the framework is the consideration of accident frequency with respect to behaviors that influence driver decisionmaking. In particular, the analysis shown here suggests that examining accident frequency alone is misleading and may minimize the impact of other important safety factors. Although the basic signal detection model is descriptive in nature, it can be refined in conjunction with field studies or laboratory experiments to provide a better understanding of driver behavior.

# 1. Introduction

## 1.1 Background

The Federal Railroad Administration (FRA) is seeking a better understanding of motor vehicle driver decisionmaking at highway-railroad grade crossings. The traditional "Three E" approach focusing on education, enforcement, and engineering has been successful at reducing grade crossing fatalities, but driver error or poor judgment continues to play a significant role in grade crossing accidents (Office of the Inspector General, 2004). Several reasons have been hypothesized to account for noncompliance, from issues associated with the technology—or lack of it—at the grade crossings themselves (e.g., insufficient illumination of the crossing, poor warning device reliability) to those inherent to the driver (e.g., the perception or expectation of long waiting times). Drivers' motivations for committing a violation are not easily captured at the time of the violation. For this reason, we were interested in (1) identifying a framework for modeling driver decisionmaking strategies to understand factors that contribute to their behavior at grade crossings, and (2) applying this model to evaluate the success of various existing or proposed countermeasures.

We selected SDT as a model because it provides a way to examine drivers' decisions with respect to the detectability of the train (*sensitivity*) and to attitudinal or motivational factors that may influence a driver's criteria for judgment (*bias*). SDT describes the operator's ability to detect a signal in a background of noise as a discrete choice task. The model assumes that there are two states of the world (signal and noise) and two possible responses ("Yes, I detect a signal" and "No, I do not") (see Egan, 1975; Green and Swets, 1974 for more information). In this context, the train serves as the *signal*, and it provides visual, auditory, and even tactile cues regarding its approach (e.g., alerting lights, train horn, vibration). Other information from the surrounding environment creates *noise* that competes with the signal, making the signal more difficult to detect (e.g., flashing lights at the crossing, sounds from inside the vehicle). If the magnitude of the signal and the noise are equal, detectability is zero. As the disparity between signal and noise increases, so does detectability. This is often expressed as the signal-to-noise ratio (S/N). When signal and noise are equal, S/N =1 and detectabilty is zero. As S/N increases, detectability increases. Bias reflects the operator's tendency to say "yes" or "no". If signals are rare, the operator's expectation to see a signal will be low, and the operator's tendency will be to say "no". If signals are frequent, the operator's expectation to see a signal will be high, and the operator's tendency will be to say "yes". Motivation also affects bias. For example, if the decision to say "yes" costs the operator money, the operator's tendency will be to say "no". If the decision to say "yes" benefits the operator (the operator gains money), the operator's tendency will be to say "yes". Both sensitivity and bias influence the driver in deciding what action to take.

Thus, the two states of the world are that there is a train approaching the grade crossing or there is not. The driver can then respond in one of two ways: stop or proceed. This situation creates four decision-event related outcomes, as described by the signal-response matrix in Table 1. The impact of compliant behavior at a grade crossing is indicated by the bold text in each of the four cells. A **valid stop** describes the decision to stop when a train is close; this is considered a *hit* in SDT. A **correct crossing** is the decision to proceed when a train is not approaching, a *correct rejection* in SDT. In some cases, a driver may think a train is approaching when one is not and stop unnecessarily, a *false alarm* in SDT and characterized here as a **false stop**. Of concern is the potential for an **accident**, the failure to stop for a train when one is approaching, either by error or intention. In the SDT framework, this is described as a *miss*.

The signal and noise distributions are generally described as two theoretic normal distributions to capture the different perceptual magnitudes from one presentation to another, as shown in Figure 1.

The *signal* distribution on the right represents the probability that a train is approaching the crossing whereas the noise distribution on the left represents the probability that there is no train. *Sensitivity* (d') reflects one's ability to discriminate between signal and noise, and it is described as the difference between the means of the signal and noise distributions. The further apart the two distributions are, the easier it is for a driver to detect whether a train is approaching. *Bias* ($\beta$) reflects a driver's tendency to stop or proceed, and it is depicted by the solid gray vertical line in the figure. A shift to the left demonstrates conservative behavior; that is, the driver is more likely to respond "stop," which increases the number of valid stops, but unfortunately also the number of false stops.

**Table 1. Signal-Response Matrix for a Driver at a Grade Crossing**

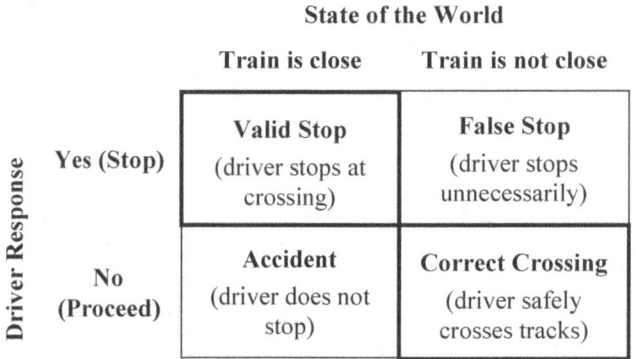

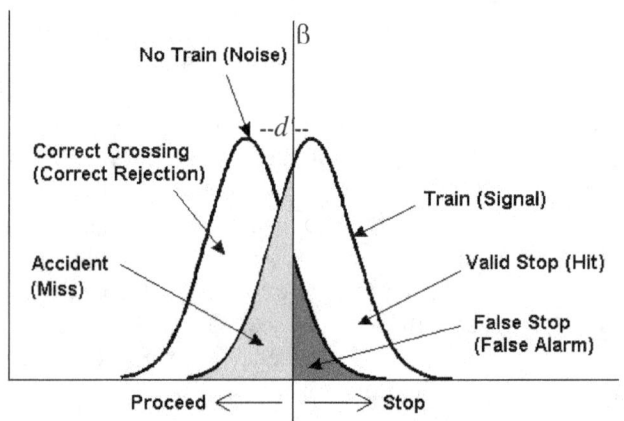

**Figure 1. Signal and Noise Probability Distributions**

Raslear (1996) applied SDT to grade crossing accidents that occurred in 1986 to examine the effectiveness of eight types of grade crossing warning devices and to determine whether their effectiveness was because they increased the signal-to-noise ratio (*sensitivity*), whether they encouraged drivers to stop (*bias*), or some combination of the two components. Four devices constituted passive warning systems— no protection, the crossbuck, stop sign, or other signs or signals—classified as such because the information they provide does not change regardless of the presence or approach of a train. Four devices constituted active warning systems: gates, flashing lights, highway traffic signals, and special warning devices. Device effectiveness was derived for each warning device as a ratio of the accident risk at a grade crossing (maximum probability of an accident) relative to the observed probability of an accident. If the maximum probability of an accident is equal to the observed probability of an accident, the effectiveness ratio is one and the device is neutral in effectiveness.

The results indicated that all warning devices are effective primarily because of how they influence drivers to stop. Bias was highly correlated with device effectiveness, accounting for approximately 60 percent of the variance in the effectiveness of the devices. Active grade crossing warning devices were more effective than passive warning devices, with gates having the highest bias of all the warning systems. Grade crossings with no protection were the least effective; the estimation of bias was greater than 1 ($\beta = 1.45$), suggesting that drivers were more likely to proceed than to stop. Sensitivity was relatively high overall, suggesting that the train presents a tremendous signal relative to environmental noise; it differed little across the eight warning devices types.

We were interested in updating the analysis conducted by Raslear (1996). By comparing accident data from 2007 (the most current year available when this effort began) with the findings from the initial study, we hoped to understand the changes over time in driver decisionmaking. Since 1986 when the original analysis was conducted, several countermeasures were implemented in an effort to improve safety at grade crossings. If the model was applicable to the grade crossing problem, we expected to see improvements in drivers' sensitivity and/or a conservative shift in their response criterion corresponding to the drop in accident rate during the time period examined. We also wanted to evaluate the robustness of the framework by empirically examining the predictions of the SDT model to understand the effects of previous safety improvements.

The next three chapters of this report (Sections 2 through 4) describe our application of the SDT model to driver decisionmaking at grade crossings and our empirical test of the framework. Section 2 describes our test of the model and our empirical findings when comparing data from 2007 to that from 1986. On the basis of this test, we made some adjustments to our assumptions in setting up the model, and we applied this revised framework to conduct a more detailed historical analysis of driver decisionmaking at grade crossings, as described in Section 3. Section 4 describes our test of the robustness of the SDT model and our application of SDT to predict the effect of proposed countermeasures.

We were also interested in developing a theoretical model to test the predictive abilities of the SDT framework through performance by an *ideal observer*. This discussion is presented in Section 5. Whereas the previous sections examine the empirical changes in sensitivity and bias over time and with changes in the grade crossing environment, Section 5 posits theoretical mechanisms for those changes and compares theoretical outcomes with actual outcomes.

Finally, Section 6 addresses the implications of the collective analyses and proposes considerations and next steps for future research.

## 2.    A Comparison of Driver Decisionmaking:  1986 and 2007

The purpose of this analysis was to test the applicability of SDT to driver decisionmaking at grade crossings by estimating the effectiveness of eight types of warning devices and examining whether they were effective because they increased the signal-to-noise ratio or because they encouraged drivers to stop. We updated the analysis conducted by Raslear (1996) using 2007 data and compared the findings between the 2 years to understand the model's predictions regarding the changes in driver decisionmaking.

### 2.1    Methods

We estimated sensitivity, bias, and device effectiveness for eight grade crossing warning device types, as shown in Table 2.

Table 2:

**Table 2.  Grade Crossing Warning Devices**

| Warning Type | Type of Protection |
|---|---|
| Passive | • no protection<br>• other signs or signals<br>• crossbuck<br>• stop sign |
| Active | • special warning devices (e.g., manually operated signals or gates, watchmen, floodlights, train crew flagging the crossing)<br>• other train activated warning devices (e.g., highway traffic signals, wigwags)<br>• flashing lights<br>• gates (including four-quadrant gates) |

The first four warning devices are considered passive warning devices, and the last four are active warning devices.

We estimated sensitivity using d', which was calculated as:

$$d' = z[P(VS)] - z[P(FS)]. \qquad (1)$$

In the formula, P(VS) is the probability of a valid stop (a hit), P(FS) is the probability of a false stop (a false alarm) and z is the unit normal distribution transform.  d' can have values that range from zero (no sensitivity to differences between signal and noise) to infinity (infinite sensitivity).  We estimated bias using β, which was calculated as:

6

$$\beta = \frac{y(VS)}{y(FS)}, \tag{2}$$

where

$$y(VS) = 0.3989e^{-z[P(VS)]^2/2}, \tag{3}$$

and

$$y(FS) = 0.3989e^{-z[P(FS)]^2/2} \tag{4}$$

When $\beta = 1$, there is no bias. Values of $\beta < 1$ indicate a bias to stop, and values of $\beta > 1$ indicate a bias to proceed.

The values for P(VS) and P(FS) were estimated from accident data, as described in Raslear (1996). By definition, P(VS) is equal to 1 minus the probability of an accident (i.e., $1 - P(AC)$). P(AC) can be calculated from the accident rate for each warning device, normalized for exposure. Each warning device is used at a different number of crossings, and each of these crossings is frequented by a different number of trains per day and a different number of motor vehicles per day. Grade crossing warning devices are selected by States depending on the number of trains per day and cars per day at the crossing and other relevant factors, so active warning devices that offer more information about whether a train is approaching will also have higher exposure than passive warning devices. To take these factors into consideration, P(AC) was calculated as the accident rate per crossing per train per highway vehicle per minute (min) for each grade crossing warning device.

P(FS) was not as straightforward to define as P(VS). To do so, we estimated the probability of a correct crossing, P(CC), and then calculated P(FS) as 1 minus P(CC). P(CC) reflects the probability that a car and a train will arrive at the crossing at the same time and that one (or both) will stop. To estimate P(CC), we quantified the reverse; that is, the probability that a car and a train will arrive at the grade crossing at the same time and that neither can stop. We described this estimate as the maximum accident risk at a grade crossing, $P(AC)_{max}$. P(CC) is thus equal to 1 minus $P(AC)_{max}$. Therefore:

$$P(FS) = 1 - P(CC) = 1 - [1 - P(AC)_{max}] = P(AC)_{max} \tag{5}$$

In other words, P(FS) is equal to the accident risk associated with each warning device.

It is worth mentioning that by estimating P(FS) as the accident risk, we characterize "conservative" behavior differently from other SDT models. Conservative behavior generally reflects a reluctance to recognize that a signal is present (i.e., a greater tendency to say "no"), but it is based on an estimate of P(FS) that reflects the operator's inclination to say "yes" when no signal was present. In the grade crossing model we developed here, $P(FS) = P(AC)_{max}$, and thus reflects drivers' tendency to say "no" when a train is present. As a result, in this framework, more conservative behavior reflects increased stopping behavior (i.e., a greater tendency to say "yes").

$P(AC)_{max}$ was calculated as the product of the probability that one or more trains would be observed at a grade crossing in a 1-min period ($p_T$) and the probability that one or more highway vehicles would be observed at a grade crossing in a 1-min period ($p_H$). We assumed that these two events were random, independent events that had an equal probability of happening throughout the day. If this were the case, the Poisson probability distribution could be used to model each event (see Raslear, 1996, for more detail). Therefore, the probability of each event ($p_T$, $p_H$) can be described as:

$$p_T = 1 - e^{-\lambda_T}, \tag{6}$$

and

7

$$p_H = 1 - e^{-\lambda_H}, \tag{7}$$

where $\lambda_T$ represents the mean frequency of a train at a grade crossing in a 1-min period, and $\lambda_H$ represents the mean frequency of a highway vehicle at a grade crossing in a 1-min period. $\lambda_T$ and $\lambda_H$ were estimated from the train rate per day at a crossing and the AADT at a crossing, respectively.

Finally, we wanted to measure the effectiveness of each grade crossing warning device. This was estimated by Raslear (1996) by computing the ratio between the maximum probability of an accident and the observed probability of an accident. It can be described as:

$$\text{Device Effectiveness} = \frac{P(FS)}{P(AC)} = \frac{P(AC)_{max}}{P(AC)}. \tag{8}$$

The information needed for this analysis was contained in two separate FRA databases: the Highway-Rail Grade Crossing Accident/Incident database and the National Highway-Rail Crossing Inventory[1]. The Highway-Rail Grade Crossing Accident/Incident database contains records about collisions occurring at a highway-rail grade crossing during a calendar year, so it was used to calculate the total number of events for each of the eight types of grade crossing warning devices in a given year. The accidents in the database were filtered so that only accidents occurring at a public grade crossing and involving a motor vehicle were counted. The warning device was assigned based on the strongest warning device at the crossing, as coded in the CROSSING field of the database. Each warning device is coded as a 2-digit number, and the field can contain anywhere from 2 to 24 characters (e.g., a crossing protected by gates will generally also have flashing lights, a crossbuck, and an advance warning sign).

The National Highway-Rail Crossing Inventory contains data on the physical and operating characteristics of all grade crossings, and it was used to determine the number of public grade crossings protected by each of the eight warning devices, the median number of trains per day for the crossings, and the median AADT at the crossings. The Highway-Rail Crossing Inventory is continuously updated, and a yearly snapshot can be found in FRA's *Highway-Rail Crossing Accident/Incident and Inventory Bulletin* or *Annual Report*[2]. We used data from that publication to collect information for 1986, the year that was examined by Raslear (1996). FRA's *Annual Report* for 2007 was not published at the time of this analysis, so we obtained data for 2007 from the Highway-Rail Crossing Inventory. The data used for this analysis was downloaded from FRA's Office of Safety Analysis website (safetydata.fra.dot.gov/officeofsafety/) on July 24, 2008. As noted above, the inventory database is continuously updated, so a "static" snapshot of the inventory as of December 31, 2007, was not available. Consequently, some new crossings, such as those opened in early 2008, may have been included in the analysis, and crossings closed in early 2008 may have been excluded. Given the large number of crossings, this possibility was not expected to have a significant effect on the analysis. The warning device at each crossing was identified using the WDCODE field in the inventory. For consistency, four-quad gates, identified in the Highway-Rail Crossing Inventory, were counted with gates, since the accidents calculated from the Highway-Rail Grade Crossing Accident/Incident database do not distinguish between the two warning devices.

One problem with the Highway-Rail Crossing Inventory is that the fields for trains per day and AADT may not be updated each year. Consequently, a comparison of the median AADT in 1986 with that in 2007 showed a *decrease* for some warning devices (see Appendix A). This finding seemed contrary to other information that suggested there should be an overall increase in AADT (e.g., the number of

---

[1] 49 CFR 225 requires that any impact between a roadway user and a piece of on track equipment be reported.

[2] The FRA stopped publishing the *Highway-Rail Crossing Accident/Incident and Inventory Bulletin* in 1996. In 1997 and subsequent years, the information is provided in the *Annual Report*.

highway vehicles and national vehicle miles travelled (VMT) increased in that same time period; see the Federal Highway Administration's (FHWA) *Highway Statistics* series). Therefore, we were concerned with the reliability of the measures used to equalize for exposure, and we looked for ways to adjust our estimates.

We used information regarding the overall number of trains to capture changes in the train rate per day at a grade crossing from 1986 to 2007. FRA and the American Association of Railroads (AAR) provide data on the number of train miles traveled and the number of track miles for each year; we used the data for 1986 through 2007. The number of trains can be obtained by dividing those two values. The 1986 rate for trains per day from the Highway-Rail Crossing Inventory was not changed for our analysis. Rather, we adjusted our estimation of the frequency of encountering a train at a grade crossing for 2007 by using the 1986 rate from the Highway-Rail Crossing Inventory as a baseline; we then increased the train rate per day for each warning device in 2007 proportionally as a function of the increase in the number of trains since 1986. We hoped that this calculation would capture the changes in exposure while minimizing the effect of any error in the train rate per day reported for 1986 in the Highway-Rail Grade Crossing Inventory.

We used a similar process to estimate changes in the highway vehicle rate. We collected information on national VMT from 1987 through 2007 from the FHWA *Highway Statistics* series. The AADT for 1986 reported in the Highway-Rail Crossing Inventory was unchanged for the analysis and it served as our baseline for proportionally increasing the AADT based on the change in VMT for each warning device for 2007.[3]

## 2.2   Results

The estimations for d' and $\beta$ in 2007 for seven of the eight grade crossing warning devices are shown in Table 3. The estimates for warning devices in the "other signs or signals" category could not be calculated because there were no accidents at those crossings in that year; consequently, P(VS) equaled one, and z[P(VS)] approached infinity.

**Table 3.  2007 estimates for d' and $\beta$**

| Warning Type | Warning Device | 2007 d' | Beta |
|---|---|---|---|
| Passive | No Signs or Signals | 7.54 | 0.0710 |
| | Other Signs or Signals* | -- | -- |
| | Crossbucks | 7.24 | 0.0317 |
| | Stop Signs | 7.03 | 0.0743 |
| Active | Special Active Warning Devices | 7.41 | 0.0017 |
| | Highway Traffic Signals, Wigwags, Bells, or Other Activated Warning Devices | 7.06 | 0.0027 |
| | Flashing Lights | 7.17 | 0.0005 |
| | Gates | 6.93 | 6.58E-05 |
| | **AVERAGE** | **7.20** | **0.026** |

\* **Since no accidents occurred for "Other Signs or Signals," values for d' and Beta could not be calculated.**

---

[3] The analysis with actual data is included in Appendix A.

As Table 3 shows, the mean d' for all warning devices was 7.20, with higher estimates for passive warning systems than active warning systems. The highest estimate was for crossings with no signs or signals (7.54) and the lowest was for gates (6.93)[4]. The results make intuitive sense; grade crossings with no signs, signals, or barriers generate less perceptual "noise" that compete for the driver's attention, so the signal-to-noise ratio may be greater and the train more detectable.

However, a high signal-to-noise ratio indicates only that the train is detectable but does not guarantee that drivers will stop. In fact, the estimates for β suggest that drivers were more likely to stop at grade crossings protected with active warning systems than at those protected with passive warning systems. The mean estimate for β was 0.026. Drivers exhibited the most conservative behavior at grade crossings with gates and the most risky behavior at grade crossings protected by stop signs only or at those with no signs or signals.

We were interested in comparing the 2007 estimations with the 1986 estimates reported by Raslear (1996). However, we wanted to first develop an estimate for the "other signs and signals" category of warning devices. We considered using nonparametric estimations for d' and β (such as A' and B", respectively (see Grier, 1971)), but they were not robust enough to capture the changes adequately because they were more limited in range. Instead, we chose to conduct a data swap by subtracting an accident from a similar warning device and adding that accident to "Other Signs or Signals". The number of accidents for "Other Signs or Signals" would now contain one accident, which would allow d' and β to be estimated, even though the actual value would not be as large for d' or as small for β as it would have been if an estimate could have been derived for no accidents. At the same time, the number of accidents for the warning device from which the accident was borrowed would decrease by one and show a slight increase in d' and decrease in beta.

The results of the swap are provided in Table 4, with data from 1986 included for comparison. We also included an estimate for device effectiveness for each warning device in Table 4. Device effectiveness represents the ratio of the accident risk at a grade crossing relative to the observed probability of an accident that occurred in 1986. To conduct the swap, we borrowed one accident from the crossbuck category and placed it into "Other Signs or Signals," as indicated by the highlighted cells. We chose the crossbuck for two reasons. First, we wanted to borrow an accident from a similar type device, and both "other signs or signals" and "crossbucks" are passive warning devices. Second, the crossbuck had the highest number of accidents for passive warning devices, and we hypothesized that borrowing an accident from the warning device with the most accidents would have the least effect on altering the estimation of d' and beta for that warning device. In fact, a comparison of Table 3 and Table 4 shows virtually no change in the estimate of d' for the crossbuck and a small change (0.0002 points) in the estimate for β.

---

[4] To provide some perspective concerning what the magnitude of d' values mean, if d' = 0, an observer would correctly say that a 1kHz tone at the threshold of human hearing (0 decibels (dB)) was audible in an anechoic chamber (0 dB) 50% of the time. If d' = 2, that observer would correctly say that a conversation (at 60 dB) was audible in a quiet room (at 40 dB) 97.7% of the time. If d' = 7, that observer would say that the sound of a power lawn mower (at 95 dB) was audible on a noisy street (at 65 dB) 99.999999998% of the time. These examples are approximate and are only true if there is no bias (β = 1).

**Table 4.** 1986 and 2007 estimations for d', β, and device effectiveness. The results for 2007 reflect the results of an "accident swap"; one accident was borrowed from the crossbuck category and used for other signs and signals so that d' and β could be estimated for that warning device.

| Warning device | 1986 | | | 2007 | | |
|---|---|---|---|---|---|---|
| | d' | β | Device Effectiveness | d' | β | Device Effectiveness |
| No Signs or Signals | 7.40 | 1.4865 | 0.66 | 7.54 | 0.0710 | 16.6420 |
| Other Signs or Signals | 6.98 | 1.0330 | 0.97 | 7.58 | 0.0079 | 171.1196 |
| Crossbucks | 7.12 | 0.6736 | 1.53 | 7.24 | 0.0315 | 40.1290 |
| Stop Signs | 6.34 | 8.2398 | 0.10 | 7.03 | 0.0743 | 16.2039 |
| Special Active Warning Devices | 7.28 | 0.0222 | 58.10 | 7.41 | 0.0017 | 866.6327 |
| Highway Traffic Signals, Wigwags, Bells, or Other Activated Warning Devices | 6.68 | 0.1497 | 7.75 | 7.06 | 0.0027 | 568.3627 |
| Flashing Lights | 6.96 | 0.0099 | 141.18 | 7.17 | 0.0005 | 3560.0559 |
| Gates | 6.84 | 0.0010 | 1667.92 | 6.93 | 6.58E-05 | 31444.8916 |
| **AVERAGE** | 6.95 | 1.45 | 234.77 | 7.24 | 0.024 | 4585.50 |

The two data sets are plotted below in Figure 2 on a transformed Receiver-Operator Characteristic (ROC) curve of z(VS) versus z(FS). Data for 1986 are drawn in gray and data for 2007 are in black.

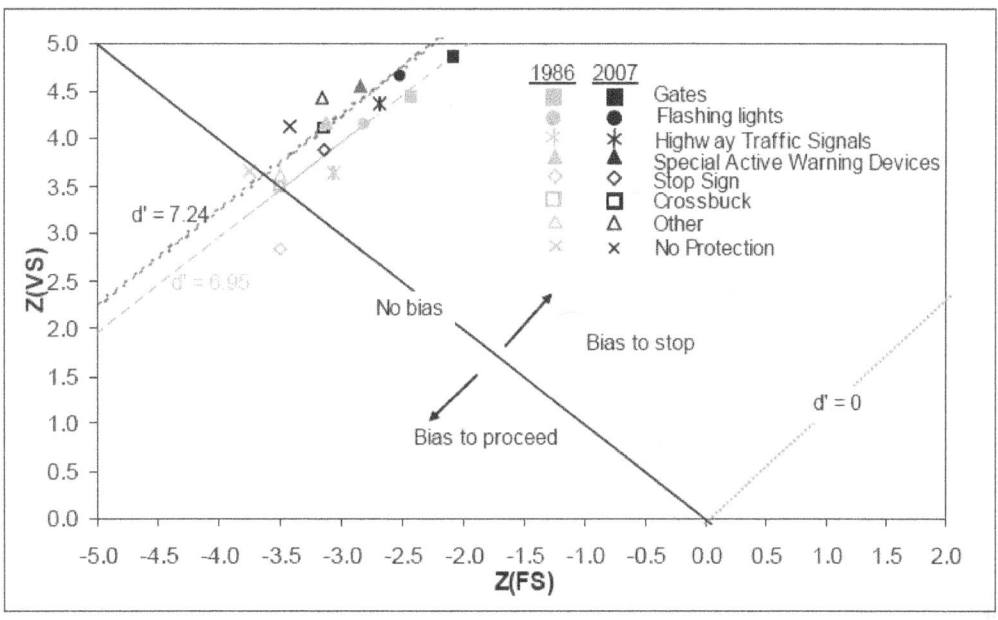

**Figure 2. ROC plots for 1986 and 2007**

Both Table 4 and Figure 2 show that estimations of d' were fairly high for both years (6.95 in 1986 and 7.24 in 2007), suggesting that the train presents a fairly salient signal at a grade crossing. Estimates of sensitivity were highest for crossings with no signs or signals and lowest at crossings with stop signs. Proportionally, the change in sensitivity throughout the 21 years was approximately 4 percent for all the warning devices combined, with the greatest individual increase (11 percent) observed for the stop sign. Even small changes in d' could increase or decrease accidents by an order of magnitude (see Raslear, 1996), and the overall change found here was statistically reliable: $t(7) = 3.54$, $p < 0.05$. The mean d' for each year is drawn in Figure 2 using the dotted lines. A third line, extending from the origin (0, 0) to the right illustrates zero sensitivity (d' = 0). The figure shows z(VS) versus z(FS) rather than P(VS) versus P(FS), so the sensitivity contours are straight lines with a slope of one. In the figure, the data points for each warning device for a given year fall fairly close to the mean for that year, indicating that there was little difference in the signal-to-noise ratio across the warning devices.

The change in $\beta$ can also be seen in Figure 2. A value of $\beta = 1$ represents no bias (in Figure 2, this is depicted as the solid diagonal extending from the top left to point (0, 0)), a value of $\beta < 1$ indicates a bias to stop (the area above the diagonal), and a value of $\beta > 1$ indicates a bias to proceed (the area below the diagonal). The average $\beta$ in 1986 was 1.45, indicating that drivers were more likely to proceed than to stop, but much of this risky behavior reflected decisions at passive grade crossings. In 2007, drivers were more likely to stop than proceed at a grade crossing; this conservative change in driver decisionmaking can be seen in a shift up and to the right for each of the warning devices, and all the data points fall above the solid diagonal where $\beta = 1$. In fact, the estimations of $\beta$ improved from 1986 values by 60 times to an average of 0.024. A comparison of $\beta$ across the 2 years, using the natural logarithm, indicated that this shift was statistically reliable, $t(7) = 10.94$, p < 0.05.

The changes in d' and $\beta$ can be considered with respect to estimations of warning device effectiveness, as shown in Table 4. As described in the previous section, device effectiveness was estimated as a ratio of the accident risk, P(FS), to the accident rate, P(AC). The more effective the warning device, the higher the ratio. Ratios less than or equal to one occur when the accident rate is higher than the accident risk, and may be a sign that a warning device is not wholly or consistently effective.

The device effectiveness ratios in Table4 show considerable improvements from 1986 through 2007. Active warning devices were more effective than passive warning devices; in 2007, the average device effectiveness ratio for active warning devices was approximately 150 times greater than the average for passive warning devices. For both years examined, gates were the most effective warning device, with a device effectiveness ratio 10 times greater than the second most effective warning device, flashing lights. The stop sign was the least effective warning device, although its effectiveness greatly improved from 1986 (0.10), when there appeared to be a greater likelihood of accidents than would be expected given the train and highway vehicle rates. Factors which account for this change are discussed in more detail in the next section.

We were interested in determining whether the effectiveness of the warning devices was attributable to changes in the signal-to-noise ratio or changes in driver's bias. To do this, we performed correlations between d' and device effectiveness and between $\beta$ and device effectiveness using the 2007 data. For the purposes of this analysis, device effectiveness was transformed using the base 10 logarithm and $\beta$ was transformed using the natural logarithm.

The results showed a statistically reliable relationship between device effectiveness and $\beta$ (r = -0.99, p < 0.05); in fact, the high value of $r$ suggests that the setting of the response criterion accounted for most of the variance in device effectiveness. On the other hand, sensitivity had little effect on device effectiveness; the correlation between device effectiveness and d' was not statistically reliable (r = -0.44, p > 0.05). The results are consistent with those reported by Raslear (1996), who concluded that the effectiveness of grade crossing warning devices appears to stem from how they influence the setting of bias in the decisionmaking process.

Thus, the results of this analysis show that safety improved at grade crossings and that much of this improvement was attributable to drivers' greater willingness to stop than proceed. One limitation of the current analysis is that it provides only two snapshots of driver behavior at grade crossings. It does not tell whether the changes in d' and β occurred suddenly or improved gradually throughout the 21-year period. We were interested in developing a more detailed picture of driver decisionmaking at grade crossings, using SDT, so we calculated d' and β for each of the intervening years. The results are described in the next section.

# 3.    Driver Decisionmaking:  1986 through 2007

We applied SDT to examine changes in sensitivity and bias for each year from 1986 to 2007.  We were interested in examining patterns of driver behavior throughout the time period to determine whether key events could be identified to account for the improvements in 2007.

## 3.1    Method

As with the previous analysis, we estimated sensitivity, bias, and device effectiveness for eight warning device types:  no protection, other signs or signals, crossbuck, stop sign, special warning devices, other activated warning devices (e.g., highway traffic signals, wigwags), flashing lights, and gates (including four-quadrant gates).  Sensitivity was estimated using d', bias was estimated using β, and device effectiveness was estimated as the ratio of the maximum probability of an accident to the observed probability of an accident.  The formulas are described in Section 2.1.

The probability of a valid stop, P(VS), was estimated as $1 - P(AC)$, with P(AC) defined as the accident rate per crossing per train per highway vehicle per minute.  The false alarm rate, P(FS), was estimated as $P(AC)_{max}$, the accident risk associated with each warning device.

We calculated the number of accidents for each warning device for each year from 1986 through 2007 using data from the Highway-Rail Grade Crossing Accident/Incident database; a spreadsheet for each year can be downloaded from FRA's Office of Safety Web site.  As was done in the previous analysis, the accidents in the database were filtered to count only those occurring at a public grade crossing and involving a motor vehicle.  The warning device was assigned according to the strongest warning device listed in the CROSSING field.

The number of public crossings at which each warning device was installed was collected from the National Highway-Rail Crossing Inventory.  Data for the years 1986 through 1996 were provided in yearly snapshots in FRA's *Highway-Rail Crossing Accident/Incident and Inventory Bulletin*, published for that specific year.  FRA stopped producing the bulletins in 1997, and instead published the *Railroad Safety Statistics Annual Report*, which provided similar information.  These annual reports were the source for data for the years 1997 through 2006.  The annual report for 2007 was not yet published when the analysis was conducted, so we downloaded data from the Highway-Rail Crossing Inventory to calculate the number of public grade crossings at which each warning device was used.  The data was downloaded on July 24, 2008, so some new crossings opened in early 2008 may have been included, and crossings closed in early 2008 may have been excluded, but we did not expect these small changes to have a significant effect on the analysis given the large number of grade crossings.

However, we were concerned with the currency of the data reported in the Highway-Rail Crossing Inventory for trains per day and AADT for each crossing.  As described in the previous section, the trend in trains per day and AADT did not seem consistent with other information showing increases in train miles travelled and vehicle miles travelled.  Therefore, we derived estimates for the train and highway vehicle rates ($\lambda_T$ and $\lambda_H$) for each warning device for each year from 1987 through 2007 by proportionally increasing the median trains per day and median AADT values for 1986 as a function of the change in the number of trains and VMT, respectively (see Section 2.1 for more information).  By basing these estimates for exposure using data from the Highway-Rail Crossing Inventory for only 1986, we hoped that we could reflect the changes in exposure while minimizing the effect of any reporting error.

## 3.2    Results

Figure 3 presents the estimates for d' for each warning device for each year throughout the 21-year period.  There were no accidents for the warning device "Other Signs or Signals" in 2004 or 2007, so d' was estimated for those years using the mean over the other years.  The thick gray line in the figures represents the average d' estimate for each year. Figure 4 plots the overall mean, median, minimum, and maximum estimates for each warning device from 1986 through 2007; the values are listed in Table 5.

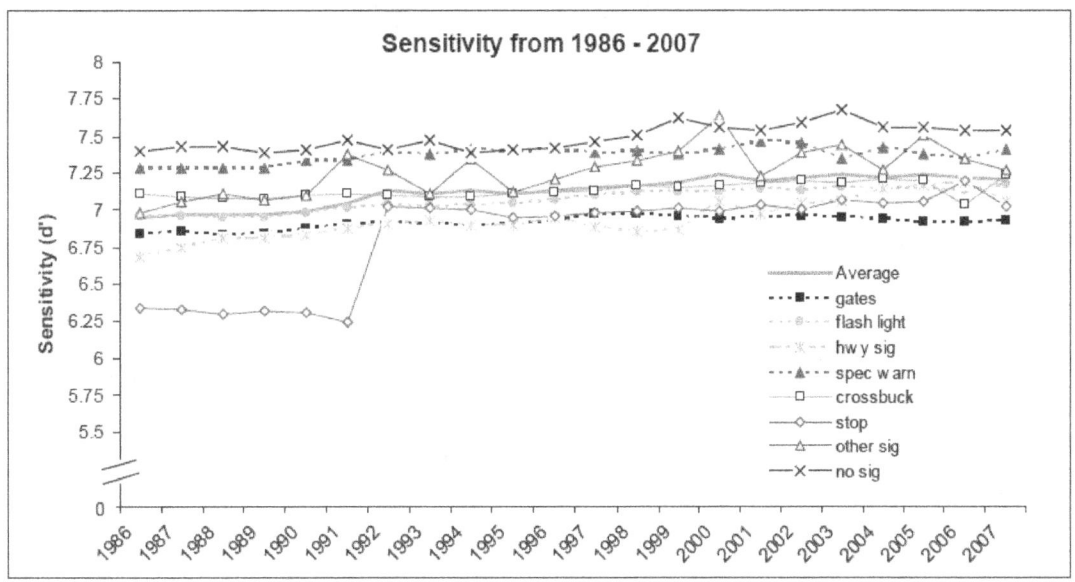

Figure 3. d' from 1986 through 2007

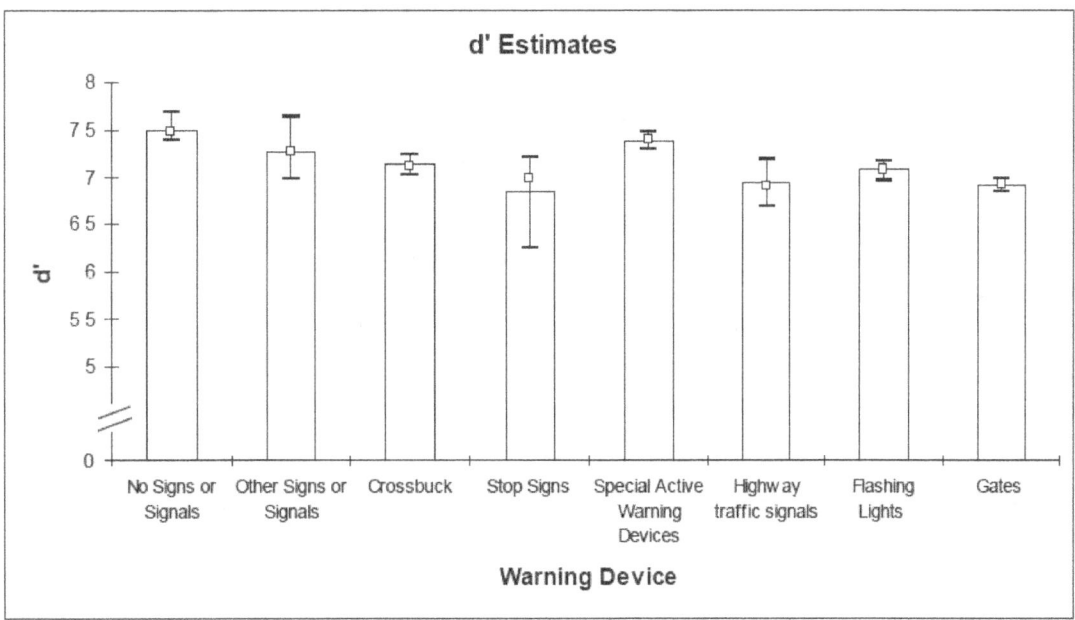

Figure 4. Plot of the Mean, Median, Minimum, and Maximum d' Estimates by Warning Device (1986–2007). Note: In the figure, the mean is depicted by the white bars, and the median is indicated with square symbols.

**Table 5. Mean, Median, Minimum, and Maximum d' Estimates by Warning Device (1986–2007)**

| Warning Device | Mean | Median | Minimum | Maximum |
|---|---|---|---|---|
| No Signs or Signals | 7.49 | 7.48 | 7.39 | 7.68 |
| Other Signs or Signals | 7.27 | 7.27 | 6.98 | 7.64 |
| Crossbucks | 7.13 | 7.12 | 7.03 | 7.24 |
| Stop Signs | 6.83 | 7.00 | 6.25 | 7.20 |
| Special Active Warning Devices | 7.37 | 7.39 | 7.28 | 7.47 |
| Highway Traffic Signals, Wigwags, Bells, or Other Activated Warning Devices | 6.94 | 6.91 | 6.68 | 7.19 |
| Flashing Lights | 7.07 | 7.08 | 6.95 | 7.17 |
| Gates | 6.91 | 6.92 | 6.83 | 6.97 |

As Figure 3 shows, sensitivity increased steadily throughout the years, ranging from a low of 6.95 in 1986 to a high of 7.24 in 2005. We used a 22 (year) x 8 (warning device) Analysis of Variance (ANOVA) to determine if the changes were statistically reliable for each variable. (Note that because there was only one observation for each warning device each year, the interaction was not included in the model.) The results showed that although the change each year was small, the effect of year was statistically reliable, $F(21, 147) = 5.82$, $p < 0.01$. The warning devices also differed in their sensitivity, $F(7, 147) = 89.25$, $p < 0.05$. Of all eight warning devices, crossings with no signs or signals generally had the highest estimates for d', with an average of 7.49 in the time period examined. Only three of the warning devices had an average d' below 7.0 in the 21-year period examined: stop sign (6.83), gates (6.91), and crossings protected by highway signals (6.94).

Of the eight warning devices, the stop sign showed the greatest improvement in sensitivity over the 21-year period examined. Although the mean d' for the stop sign was indeed lower than that for the other warning devices, the trend shown in Figure 3 suggests this was primarily due to low sensitivity in the six years from 1986 to 1991. In that time period, the average d' for the stop sign was only 6.31. In 1992, however, sensitivity improved sharply, with the estimate of d' increasing by over seven-tenths of a point to 7.03. In fact, over the 21 years examined in this analysis, estimates of d' for the stop sign changed by almost one point from 6.25 (in 1991) to 7.20 (in 2006). The changes in d' for other warning devices showed less variation over the same time period, as noted in Table 5.

Turning to β, Figure 5 presents the estimates for each warning device from 1986 through 2007. As noted previously, there were no accidents for the warning device "Other Signs or Signals" in 2004 or 2007, so β was estimated as the mean over the other years. Because β is non-linear, the changes are better depicted by transforming the estimates using the natural logarithm. The thick gray line in the figure represents the average value of ln β for each year. Table 6 lists the mean, median, minimum, and maximum estimates of ln β for each warning device over the 21-year period.

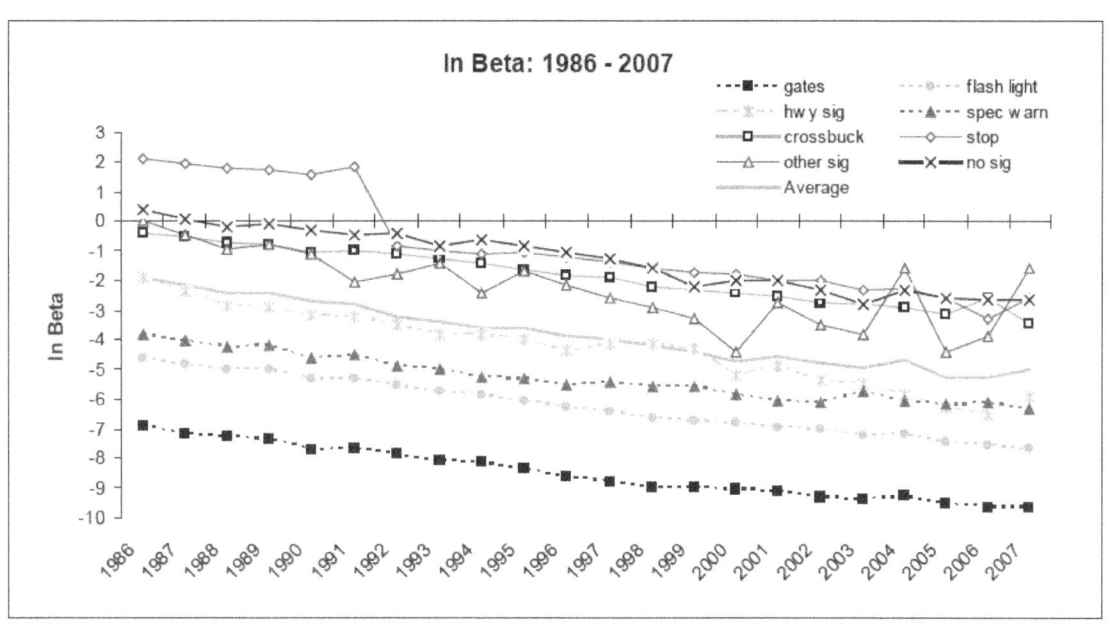

Figure 5. ln β from 1986 to 2007

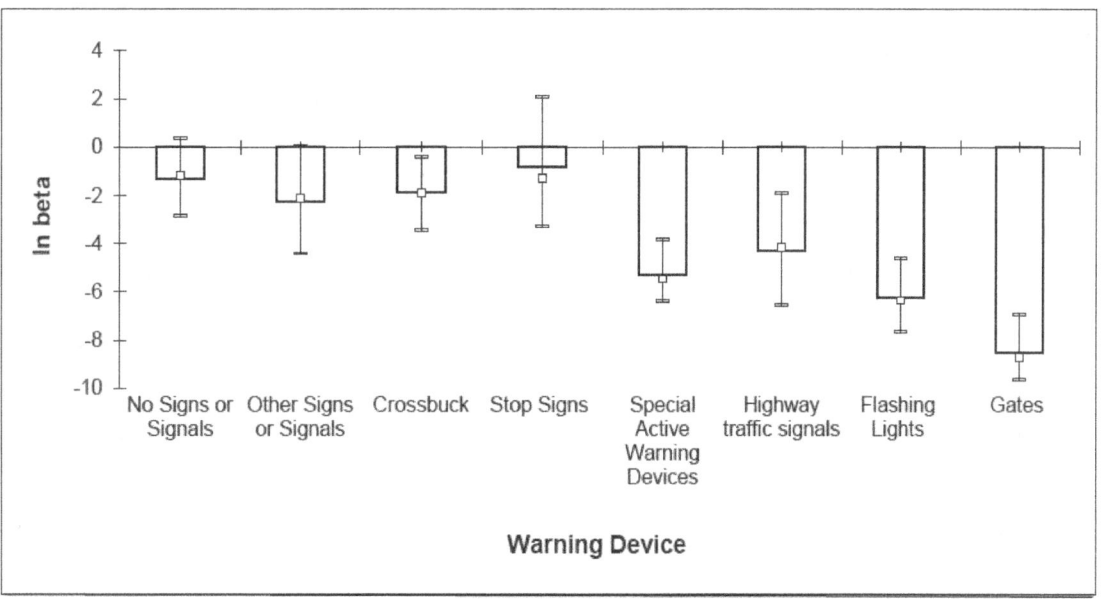

Figure 6. Plot of the Mean, Median, Minimum, and Maximum ln β values by Warning Device (1986–2007). Note: In the figure, the mean is depicted by the white bars, and the median is indicated with square symbols.

**Table 6. Mean, Median, Minimum, and Maximum Estimates of ln β by Warning Device (1986–2007)**

| Warning Device | Average | Median | Minimum | Maximum |
|---|---|---|---|---|
| No Signs or Signals | -1.31 | -1.16 | -2.81 | 0.40 |
| Other Signs or Signals | -2.25 | -2.13 | -4.41 | 0.03 |
| Crossbucks | -1.86 | -1.88 | -3.45 | -0.40 |
| Stop Signs | -0.81 | -1.30 | -3.27 | 2.11 |
| Special Active Warning Devices | -5.29 | -5.46 | -6.35 | -3.81 |
| Highway Traffic Signals, Wigwags, Bells, or Other Activated Warning Devices | -4.27 | -4.14 | -6.52 | -1.90 |
| Flashing Lights | -6.24 | -6.34 | -7.64 | -4.61 |
| Gates | -8.49 | -8.70 | -9.64 | -6.90 |

Figure 5 shows that by the end of the 21-year period examined, all the warning devices encouraged drivers to stop. In the figure, the x-axis designates where ln β = 0 and thus represents no bias (i.e., β = 1). Negative values of ln β reflect conservative behavior (that is, drivers who were more likely to stop than proceed). Positive values indicate risky behavior (that is, drivers who were more likely to proceed than stop). A 22 (year) x 8 (warning device) ANOVA, conducted using ln β, showed a statistically reliable effect of year, $F(21, 147) = 40.55$, $p < 0.05$ and warning device, $F(7, 147) = 734.13$, $p < 0.05$. (As with the previous analysis, the interaction of year and warning device was not included in the model because there was only one observation per cell.) Figure 5 also highlights the fact that drivers were more likely to stop at grade crossings protected by active warning devices (the bottom four lines in the figure) than passive warning devices (the top four lines). This behavior was fairly consistent throughout the time period examined. The most conservative behavior was observed at crossings protected by gates (the filled squares at the bottom of the figure), with an average β of $2.97 \times 10^{-4}$ (ln β = -8.49). The riskiest behavior was observed at crossings protected by stop signs (the diamonds at the top of the figure), with an average β over the 21-year period of 1.86 (ln β = -0.81). In fact, the data shows that prior to 1992, drivers were more likely to proceed than stop at crossings protected by stop signs (β > 1; ln β > 0). Similar to the pattern of change found for the estimates of d' for the stop sign, driver behavior improved sharply in 1992 relative to the previous years as drivers became much more conservative; this was reflected in a drop in β from 6.22 in 1991 to 0.43 (the change in ln β as shown in Figure 5 was from 1.83 in 1991 to -0.85 in 1992). In fact, of the eight warning devices, the estimates for β at stop sign protected crossings showed the greatest improvement—over 200 percent, ranging from a high of 8.24 in 1986 to a low of 0.04 in 2006. Due to the large variation, the median estimate for β for stop signs (0.27) may be a more descriptive estimate of driver decisionmaking, as it captures the general pattern towards stopping reflected in the data from 1992 onward. The least amount of change was found for crossings with crossbucks or no signs or signals.

We also estimated the effectiveness of each warning device for each year. The results are shown on a logarithmic scale in Figure 7; the thick gray line in the figure marks the mean across all warning devices for each year. No accidents occurred at grade crossings protected by "Other Signs or Signals" in 2004 or 2007, so its device effectiveness for those years was estimated using the mean over the other years.

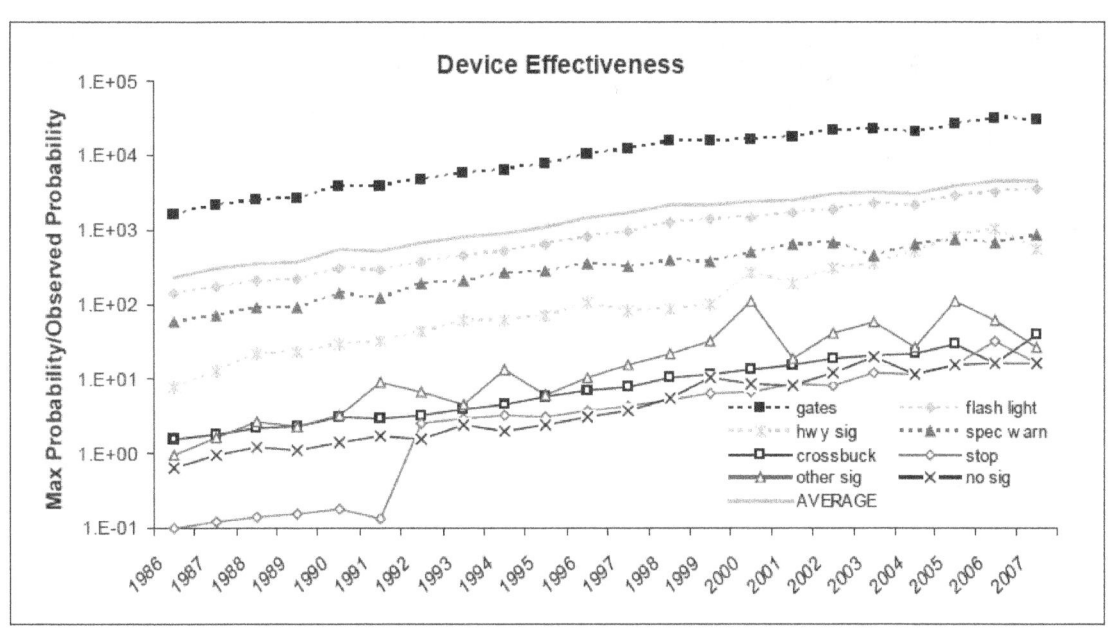

**Figure 7. Device Effectiveness: 1986 through 2007**

As the figure shows, device effectiveness showed a statistically reliable improvement from 1986 through 2007, $F(21, 147) = 48.67$, $p < 0.05$. Device effectiveness also differed considerably across the eight grade crossing warning devices, $F(7, 147) = 855.02$, $p < 0.05$. Gates had the highest device effectiveness ratio, and its effectiveness was an order of magnitude greater than the second most effective warning device, flashing lights. Device effectiveness was lowest for the stop sign (6.60) followed by crossings with no signs or signals (6.70). For both these warning devices, data from the first few years of this analysis shows a device effectiveness ratio less than one, indicating that the rate of accidents was higher than that predicted by the accident risk. For the stop sign, the device effectiveness ratio rose above one in 1992, and for crossings with no signs or signals, the device effectiveness ratio rose above one in 1988. Of the eight warning devices, device effectiveness for the stop sign improved the most in the time period examined, much of it due to a sharp reduction in the accident risk in 1992. In fact, from 1991 to 1992, the device effectiveness of the stop sign improved 18 fold from 0.14 to 2.48.

We wanted to determine whether the warning devices' effectiveness could be attributed to increased driver sensitivity or to a shift in drivers' decisionmaking, so we assessed correlations between the device effectiveness ratio for each warning device and the estimates for d' and ln β. The results showed a near-perfect correlation between device effectiveness and ln β ($r = -0.99$, $p < 0.01$) and no relationship between device effectiveness and d' ($r = -0.25$, $p > 0.05$). Thus, the effectiveness of a warning device appears to be the result of whether it encourages drivers to stop at the crossing.

One pattern that emerged from the analysis was the apparently sudden and sharp improvement in drivers' behavior at stop-sign protected crossings. To understand contributing factors to this improvement, we examined the variables used to measure exposure, as captured by P(AC), to determine whether any showed a similar trend (i.e., the number of crossings, train rate per day, highway vehicle rate per day). Of these, the most telling was the considerable increase in stop sign use at grade crossings in 1992, a change from approximately 900 crossings in the years prior to over 10,000 crossings in that year. This increase may be the direct result of the Intermodal Surface Transportation Efficiency Act of 1991 (ISTEA), which required that the Federal Highway Administration (FHWA) revise the Manual on Uniform Traffic Control Devices (MUTCD) to allow State and local governments to use stop or yield signs at passive grade crossings where two or more trains operated daily.

Despite the increased use of the stop sign, the number of accidents remained relatively unchanged— there was an average of 300 accidents per year from 1986 to 1992, and 298 accidents from 1992 to 2007. This is shown in Figure 8, which depicts the change in the number of stop-sign protected grade crossings and the accident rate from 1986 to 2007.

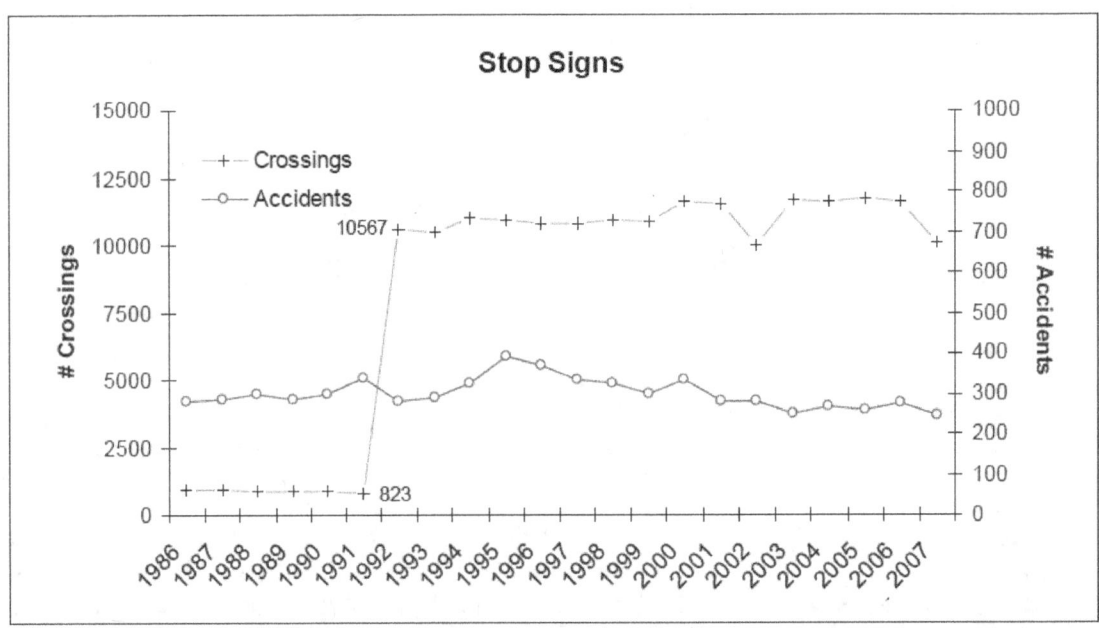

**Figure 8. The increase in the number of stop signs in 1992 did not change the accident rate.**

We investigated the correlation between the change in the number of stop sign crossings and the estimates for d' and ln β. Both sets of correlations were statistically reliable. The increase in the number of crossings *positively* correlated with the increase in sensitivity (d': $r = 0.99$, $p < 0.05$) and *negatively* correlated with the decrease in β (ln β: $r = -0.95$, $p < 0.05$). These findings by no means suggest that further increases in the use of the stop sign would improve driver decisionmaking, nor can the data be used to recommend additional use of the stop sign. Rather, the results simply reflect our estimations of the probability of an accident at a grade crossing (P(AC)), that is, the number of accidents per crossing per train per highway vehicle per minute. Thus, because the number of accidents remained relatively constant throughout the 21 years, by significantly increasing the number of crossings, P(AC) dropped considerably in 1992.

It is worth mentioning that the pattern shown in Figure 8 was atypical compared with the pattern for other warning devices. In most cases, a change in the number of crossings positively correlated with a change in the accident rate. The only exception, apart from the stop sign, was at crossings protected by gates. At these crossings, a *negative* correlation existed, such that as the number of gated crossings increased, the rate of accidents at these crossings decreased.

The overall results of the historical analysis show that improvements in safety at grade crossings were attributable to both increases in the signal-to-noise ratio and drivers' greater willingness to stop. Most of these improvements occurred steadily throughout the 21-year time period studied. Device effectiveness also improved, and this effectiveness was due primarily to a conservative shift in the response criterion. The results of the analyses demonstrate the improvements in safety noted by FRA. However, the analysis does not specifically identify what led to this improvement. We wanted to determine whether SDT could be used to identify and examine the effect of potential safety factors and quantify the impact. This was the goal of the next set of analyses.

# 4.   Safety Factors

The *2004 Audit of the Highway-Rail Grade Crossing Safety Program* (Office of the Inspector General, 2004) noted a 41 percent decrease in the number of grade crossing accidents between 1994 and 2003. A number of safety programs were implemented during this time period, and FRA was interested in measuring the relative impact of the different programs. A previous effort by Horton, et al. (2008) quantified the benefits of the different safety programs by measuring the reduction in incidents attributable to each program. We wanted to use the same approach developed by Horton, et al. but focus on the impact of those programs in terms of their effect on driver decisionmaking.

In Horton, et al. (2008), eight "successful" safety factors, selected from a greater set of safety programs identified in literature reviews and group discussions, were quantitatively evaluated. The eight factors consisted of the following:

- Improving commercial motor vehicle (CMV) driver safety (e.g., through 64 CFR §§ 383, 384)[5]
- Improving locomotive conspicuity through the use of alerting lights
- Improving the reliability of motor vehicles
- Increasing sight lines
- Improving warning device reliability
- Closing crossings and grade separation
- Upgrading warning devices
- Preempting traffic signals

Horton, et al. estimated "success" for each safety factor by comparing the percentage of incidents from 1994 through 2003 that could be attributed to a safety factor in each year and measuring the percent reduction in incidents. An incident was linked to one or more safety factors by using information provided in the data fields of the grade crossing accident reports recorded in FRA's Highway-Rail Grade Crossing Accident/Incident database. Of the eight safety factors, the initial results suggested that two of them— regulations to improve CMV driver safety and increasing locomotive conspicuity through the use of alerting lights—had the most impact on grade crossing safety, accounting for a 53 percent and 30 percent reduction in accidents, respectively. All the other safety factors had an approximately 3–5 percent impact on reducing accidents, with the exception of preempting traffic signals which had a 2 percent impact.

One concern with this analysis was that the effect of a safety factor may have been overestimated. The data fields in FRA's Grade Crossing Accident/Incident database describing an accident can cite several factors; consequently, one accident could be attributed to multiple safety factors. For example, an accident that involved a motor vehicle that was stalled on the tracks and was hit by a train would be included in the accident count for two of the safety factors listed above: "improving locomotive conspicuity through the use of alerting lights" and "improving the reliability of motor vehicles." To address this issue, Horton, et al. conducted a second analysis, isolating the effect of each safety factor. Each incident was classified as being attributable to one safety factor, more than one safety factor, or none of the safety factors. The impact and percent reduction for each safety factor was then recalculated using only a count of those incidents attributable to one safety factor only. Horton, et al. included only five of the eight safety factors from the list above in this subsequent analysis. Two of the safety factors— "crossing closure and grade separation" and "upgrading warning devices"—were not included since the

---

[5] The Federal Motor Carrier Safety Administration (FMCSA) published the *Commercial Driver Disqualification Provision* (49 CFR §§ 383, 384) on October 21, 1999; it suspended the Commercial Drivers' Licenses (CDL) of commercial motor vehicle (CMV) drivers who violated grade crossing warning devices and imposed penalties against any motor carrier who knowingly allowed, permitted, authorized, or required a CMV driver to commit such a violation.

number of incidents associated with those factors were estimated in the previous analysis, and "preempting traffic signals" was not included because it did not have a large impact. The reduction in incidents calculated for the other five safety factors is shown in Table 7.

**Table 7. Percent Reduction of Incidents for Each *Isolated* Safety Factor**

| Factor | Reduction |
|---|---|
| Improving CMV driver safety | 34.6% |
| Increasing locomotive conspicuity through the use of alerting lights | 13.6% |
| Increasing sight lines | 3.6% |
| Improving warning device reliability | 3.1% |
| Improving the reliability of motor vehicles | 3.1% |

As the table shows, two factors, "regulations to improve CMV driver safety" and "increasing locomotive conspicuity through the use of alerting lights," accounted for approximately 48 percent of the reduction in accidents. The other three factors each accounted for a 3–4 percent change in the 10-year period examined. The cumulative percent reduction for all five factors totaled 58 percent.

In considering the five safety factors in Table 6, we expected that two would exert a primary influence on sensitivity (the use of alerting lights and increasing sight lines) and two would influence bias (improving CMV driver safety regulations and improving warning device reliability). Thus, we were interested in testing whether we could quantify their effects on driver decisionmaking through SDT. The fifth safety factor, "improving the reliability of motor vehicles," was measured on the basis of whether or not an accident involved a car that broke down or stalled on the highway tracks, so we did not expect it to exert an influence on driver decisionmaking. Instead, we added another factor that we expected to influence sensitivity: the use of reflectors to increase locomotive conspicuity.

Although we distinguished the five safety factors according to how they were expected to influence sensitivity and bias, we did not expect that the two measures would change independently. Rather, we expected that a change in one would have an observable effect on the other. For example, by improving the signal-to-noise ratio of the train at a grade crossing (*sensitivity*), the train is more detectable and thus drivers may be more likely to stop. Conversely, by encouraging drivers to be more cautious at a grade crossing (*bias*), drivers may take more time and effort to look for a train, thereby increasing sensitivity.

We estimated the effect of the five safety factors on driver decisionmaking using d' and β for the years 1986 and 2007. We used the approach developed by Horton, et al. to associate an accident with a safety factor. The criteria used are described in detail in the next section. It is important to note that this analysis was by no means a causal analysis. The accidents attributed to a safety factor were based on characteristics that were included in the Highway-Rail Grade Crossing Accident/Incident database, and it is not possible to determine through the data fields alone the degree to which one or more of these factors contributed to the accident.

## 4.1 Method

The accidents in the database were filtered to include only accidents occurring at a public grade crossing and involving a motor vehicle. We defined each of the five safety factors, using data fields provided in the Highway-Rail Grade Crossing Accident/Incident database, as follows:

- Regulations to improve CMV Driver Safety: The accidents associated with this safety factor resulted from a motor vehicle that would require a Commercial Drivers' License (CDL), as identified by the TYPEVEH field (TYPEVEH = trucks, truck-trailers, buses and school buses).
- Increasing locomotive conspicuity through the use of alerting lights: Because the use of alerting lights provides more benefit at night than during the day (Carroll, Multer, and Markos, 1995), this

safety factor was defined by accidents in which rail equipment struck a motor vehicle either at dusk, dawn, or dark. These characteristics were identified by the data fields describing visibility (VISIBLTY), railroad equipment (RREQUIP = pulling or pushing), and type of accident (TYPACC).

- Increasing train conspicuity through the use of retroreflective materials: This safety factor was defined by accidents in which rail equipment was struck by a motor vehicle either at dusk, dawn, or dark. These characteristics were identified by the data fields describing visibility (VISIBLTY), railroad equipment (RREQUIP = pulling or pushing), and type of accident (TYPACC).

- Increasing sight lines: Accidents associated with this safety factor noted one of five categories of visual obstruction at the grade crossing—a permanent structure, standing railroad equipment, topography, vegetation, and other. This information was identified through the data field describing viewing conditions (VIEW). (Two other categories captured by the VIEW field—passing train and highway vehicles—were not included because they are not easily eliminated through countermeasures.)

- Improvements in warning device reliability: This safety factor pertained only to grade crossings with active warning devices. The SIGNAL field in the database identified accidents that resulted because the warning signal malfunctioned; the malfunctions consisted of alleged and confirmed warning times that were too long or too short or when no warning was presented.

We calculated P(VS) and P(FS) for each of the eight warning devices for each safety factor. P(VS) was estimated using P(AC), which was defined to be the accident rate for each safety factor per crossing per train per highway vehicle per minute. The accident rate was estimated from the *total* number of accidents in each year associated with a safety factor (i.e., the number of accidents meeting the criteria specified for each of the safety factors listed above. See Horton, et al., for more information.). The number of crossings used to calculate P(AC) reflected the total number of crossings at which the warning device was installed in 1986 or in 2007. P(FS) was estimated as $P(AC)_{max}$, the accident risk associated with each warning device.

The number of grade crossings for each warning device was determined from FRA's *Highway-Rail Crossing Accident/Incident and Inventory Bulletin* for 1986 and from the Highway-Rail Crossing Inventory for 2007. As with the previous analyses, the train rate per day and the highway vehicle rate per day for each warning device were calculated for 1986 using the median number of trains per day at the crossings and the median AADT at the crossings, respectively, as recorded in the *Highway-Rail Crossing Accident/Incident and Inventory Bulletin*. The train rate per day and the highway vehicle rate per day were estimated in 2007 using the 1986 data as a baseline and increasing the values proportionally based on the change in number of trains and VMT, respectively (see Section 2.1 for more information).

## 4.2    Results

The estimations for d' and β are described for each safety factor (The total number of accidents attributable to each safety factor for each year is shown in Appendix B.). The safety factor and the dependent variable (d' or β) are indicated at the top of each results table.

As noted in Section 2.2, there were no accidents reported at grade crossings protected by "other signs or signals" in 2007, and as Appendix B shows, there were several other warning devices for which there were no accidents attributable to one or more of the safety factors we identified in one or both of the years we examined. To estimate d' and β when no accidents existed, we conducted a data swap by borrowing an accident from a similar warning device (as described in Section 2.2 above). The number of accidents for the borrower would equal one, allowing a value to be calculated for d' and β, although these estimates would not be as large as they would have been if one could be determined for no accidents. The warning device from which the accident was borrowed (the lender), would have one less accident, which could result in a slight increase in the estimate for d' and a slight decrease in the estimate for β. The lender and borrower are noted in the text and highlighted in orange in each table.

For each safety factor, estimates of d' and the natural logarithm of β were compared using a 2 (year) x 8 (warning device) ANOVA. Because we had only one observation per cell, the ANOVA model included only the main effects. We also calculated $\omega^2$ to determine the amount of variance accounted for by each independent variable, and conducted paired comparisons to identify differences among the warning devices. Often, the comparisons identified groups of overlapping warning devices with similar estimates for d' and ln β. Therefore, in many cases, the results did not lend themselves to identifying a warning device that was "most" or "least" sensitive or "most" or "least" likely to encourage drivers to stop.

### 4.2.1 CMV Driver Safety

Table 8 shows the estimates for d' (Table 8a) and β (Table 8b) for accidents involving a CMV driver. The estimates for 2007 reflect the results of a data swap in which one accident was borrowed from the crossbuck and lent to other signs or signals. The cells involved in the data swap are highlighted in orange. The first set of columns in the tables shows the results of paired comparisons of the warning devices; warning devices with similar means are shaded in the same color.

**Table 8. CMV driver safety. Estimates of d' and β.**

**(a) CMV Driver Safety – d'**

| Warning Device | 1986 | 2007 |
|---|---|---|
| No Signs or Signals | 7.65 | 7.77 |
| Other Signs or Signals | 7.18 | 7.58 |
| Crossbucks | 7.39 | 7.54 |
| Stop Signs | 6.66 | 7.33 |
| Special Active Warning Devices | 7.56 | 7.79 |
| Highway Traffic Signals, Wigwags, Bells, or Other Activated Warning Devices | 6.98 | 7.42 |
| Flashing Lights | 7.24 | 7.48 |
| Gates | 7.15 | 7.24 |
| AVERAGE | 7.23 | 7.52 |

**(b) CMV Driver Safety – β**

| Warning Device | 1986 | 2007 |
|---|---|---|
| No Signs or Signals | 0.580 | 0.027 |
| Other Signs or Signals | 0.498 | 0.008 |
| Crossbucks | 0.236 | 0.009 |
| Stop Signs | 3.121 | 0.022 |
| Special Active Warning Devices | 0.007 | 2.90E-04 |
| Highway Traffic Signals, Wigwags, Bells, or Other Activated Warning Devices | 0.047 | 0.001 |
| Flashing Lights | 0.003 | 1.09E-04 |
| Gates | 2.501E-04 | 1.420E-05 |
| AVERAGE | 0.562 | 0.008 |

Regulations to improve CMV driver safety contributed to a 0.29 point increase in sensitivity, from 7.23 in 1986 to 7.52 in 2007. This change was statistically reliable, $F(1, 7) = 16.93$, $p < 0.05$, $\omega^2 = 0.24$. Estimations of d' also differed reliably depending on the warning device, $F(7, 7) = 6.11$, $p < 0.05$, $\omega^2 = 0.53$. Drivers were most sensitive at grade crossings with no protection or at those with special active warning devices. Sensitivity for all warning devices was higher than for the stop sign. However, the stop sign showed the largest increase in sensitivity for this safety factor over the 21-year period examined (0.67 points). Gates showed the smallest change in sensitivity (0.09 points).

Regulations are generally intended to encourage drivers to change their behavior, and estimations of $\beta$ showed that this indeed was the effect. The data showed a conservative shift from 0.562 in 1986 to 0.008 in 2007; an ANOVA comparing $\ln \beta$ in 1986 to that in 2007 indicated that this shift was statistically reliable, $F(1, 7) = 180.39$, $p < 0.05$, $\omega^2 = 0.30$. Additionally, the analysis indicated that the inclination to stop differed depending on the warning device [$\ln \beta$: $F(7, 7) = 59.11$, $p < 0.05$, $\omega^2 = 0.68$], with drivers exhibiting the most conservative behavior at crossings protected by gates, and the riskiest behavior at crossings protected by passive warning devices. The largest shift in $\ln \beta$ occurred at crossings protected by stop signs or those protected by highway traffic signals, wigwags, bells, or other activated warning devices. The smallest change was at crossings with no signs or signals.

### 4.2.2 Alerting Lights

Table 9 shows the estimates for d' and $\beta$ using the total number of accidents with visibility conditions that could be ameliorated by alerting lights. The estimates for 2007 reflect the results of a data swap in which one accident was borrowed from the crossbuck and used to derive estimates of d' and $\beta$ for other signs or signals. This is highlighted by the orange cells. Warning devices with similar means are shaded in the same color in the first set of columns.

**Table 9. Alerting Lights. Estimates of d' and $\beta$.**

**(a) Alerting Lights – d'**

| Warning Device | 1986 | 2007 |
|---|---|---|
| No Signs or Signals | 7.64 | 7.83 |
| Other Signs or Signals | 7.14 | 7.58 |
| Crossbucks | 7.45 | 7.66 |
| Stop Signs | 6.72 | 7.44 |
| Special Active Warning Devices | 7.56 | 7.79 |
| Highway Traffic Signals, Wigwags, Bells, or Other Activated Warning Devices | 7.06 | 7.37 |
| Flashing Lights | 7.25 | 7.51 |
| Gates | 7.02 | 7.13 |
| AVERAGE | 7.23 | 7.54 |

**(b) Alerting Lights – $\beta$**

| Warning Device | 1986 | 2007 |
|---|---|---|
| No Signs or Signals | 0.602 | 0.021 |
| Other Signs or Signals | 0.582 | 0.008 |
| Crossbucks | 0.191 | 0.005 |
| Stop Signs | 2.638 | 0.014 |
| Special Active Warning Devices | 0.007 | 2.90E-04 |
| Highway Traffic Signals, Wigwags, Bells, or Other Activated Warning Devices | 0.035 | 0.001 |
| Flashing Lights | 0.003 | 9.54E-05 |
| Gates | 4.648E-04 | 2.438E-05 |
| AVERAGE | 0.507 | 0.006 |

25

The number of accidents with visibility conditions that could be ameliorated by alerting lights decreased from 1986 to 2007. As Table 9 shows, this change in the number of accidents was reflected in a statistically reliable 0.31 point increase in d' from 7.23 to 7.54, $F(1, 7) = 20.30$, $p < 0.05$, $\omega^2 = 0.25$. There was also a statistically reliable difference in d' attributable to warning device, $F(7, 7) = 6.90$, $p < 0.05$, $\omega^2 = 0.54$. Estimations for d' were highest for crossings with no signs or signals and those protected by special active warning devices. Estimations of d' were lowest for crossings protected by gates or those with stop signs.

The use of alerting lights was expected to have a positive impact on d', but the data also showed a statistically reliable conservative shift in β from 0.507 in 1986 to 0.006 in 2007 (as analyzed using ln β), $F(1, 7) = 201.08$, $p < 0.05$, $\omega^2 = 0.34$. The type of warning device also had a statistically reliable influence on drivers' tendencies to stop or proceed [ln β: $F(7, 7) = 53.85$, $p < 0.05$, $\omega^2 = 0.63$]. Paired comparisons based on the estimations of ln β identified five overlapping groups with which the warning devices could be classified. While it is not clear which warning device benefited the most from the use of alerting lights, the results of the paired comparisons suggest that drivers were more likely to stop at crossings with active warning devices than at those with passive warning devices.

### 4.2.3  Reflectors

Table 10 shows the estimates for d' and β using accidents with visibility conditions that could be ameliorated by reflectors. There were no accidents at grade crossings protected by "no signs or signals" or "other signs or signals" in 2007, so the estimates for 2007 reflect the results of two data swaps. One accident each was borrowed from two categories (crossbuck and stop signs) and loaned to "no signs or signals" and "other signs or signals" to derive an estimate of d' and β. Warning devices with similar means are indicated by shading the corresponding cells in the first set of columns with the same color.

The use of reflectors was intended to improve the detectability of a train and, as a result, was expected to increase sensitivity. Although estimations of d' increased by 0.19 points from 7.47 in 1986 to 7.66 in 2007, this difference was only marginally reliable, $F(1, 7) = 4.59$, $p < 0.10$, $\omega^2 = 0.09$. The type of warning device appeared to account for more of the change in d', $F(7, 7) = 4.18$, $p < 0.05$, $\omega^2 = 0.53$. Drivers were most sensitive at grade crossings protected by no signs or signals (an average of 8.10) and less sensitive at grade crossings protected by gates, stop signs, or highway traffic signals, wigwags, bells, or other activated warning devices.

It is worth noting that although the estimates for d' for the warning device "no signs or signals," shown in Table 10, suggest a decrease in sensitivity from 1986 to 2007 (despite reflectorization), the difference is a result of the generally low number of accidents attributable to reflectors at those crossings and to the increase in accident risk at crossings with no signs and signals from 1986 through 2007. There were three accidents at grade crossings with no signs or signals in 1986 and none in 2007. However, the risk of an accident was three times higher in 2007 than in 1986.

Although the overall change in sensitivity with the use of reflectors was only marginally reliable, there was a statistically reliable drop in β from 0.188 in 1986 to 0.003 in 2007, $F(1, 7) = 79.39$, $p < 0.05$, $\omega^2 = 0.29$ (as analyzed using ln β). Estimations of ln β also differed reliably by warning device, $F(7, 7) = 25.09$, $p < 0.05$, $\omega^2 = 0.64$. The results for the paired comparisons identified four overlapping groups of warning devices with similar means. The pattern of results suggest that drivers were more inclined to stop at crossings protected by gates and flashing lights than at other warning devices, and drivers were more inclined to proceed at crossings with passive warning devices or at active crossings with highway traffic signals, wigwags, bells, or other activated warning devices.

## Table 10. Reflectors. Estimates of d' and β.

**(a) Reflectors – d'**

| Warning Device | 1986 | 2007 |
|---|---|---|
| No Signs or Signals | 8.14 | 8.06 |
| Other Signs or Signals | 7.50 | 7.58 |
| Crossbucks | 7.63 | 7.80 |
| Stop Signs | 6.96 | 7.74 |
| Special Active Warning Devices | 7.59 | 7.71 |
| Highway Traffic Signals, Wigwags, Bells, or Other Activated Warning Devices | 7.23 | 7.42 |
| Flashing Lights | 7.40 | 7.60 |
| Gates | 7.31 | 7.38 |
| AVERAGE | 7.47 | 7.66 |

**(b) Reflectors – β**

| Warning Device | 1986 | 2007 |
|---|---|---|
| No Signs or Signals | 0.077 | 0.007 |
| Other Signs or Signals | 0.146 | 0.008 |
| Crossbucks | 0.092 | 0.003 |
| Stop Signs | 1.161 | 0.004 |
| Special Active Warning Devices | 0.006 | 0.000 |
| Highway Traffic Signals, Wigwags, Bells, or Other Activated Warning Devices | 0.018 | 0.001 |
| Flashing Lights | 0.001 | 0.000 |
| Gates | 1.165E-04 | 6.501E-06 |
| AVERAGE | 0.188 | 0.003 |

### 4.2.4 Increasing Sight Lines

Table 11 presents the estimates for d' and β using accidents with visibility conditions that could be ameliorated by improving sight lines. As the table shows, three swaps were used to calculate estimates for 2007; in that year, there were no accidents attributable to the sight lines safety factor at grade crossings protected by no signs or signals, other signs or signals, or highway traffic signals, wigwags, bells, or other activated warning device. In the swap, one accident was borrowed from the crossbuck, stop signs, and flashing lights and loaned to no signs or signals, other signs or signals, and highway traffic signals, wigwags, bells, or other activated warning device categories, respectively. Note that the accidents for passive warning devices were borrowed from other passive warning devices, and the accidents for active warning devices were borrowed from other active warning devices. The results of paired comparisons for the warning devices are shown in the first set of columns in each table. Means that are not reliably different from one another are indicated by shading the corresponding cells in the same color.

Clearing obstructions to sight lines at grade crossings was expected to increase drivers' sensitivity to a train. As Table 11 shows, estimates of d' increased by 0.27 points in the time period examined, $F(1, 7) = 5.36$, $p = 0.05$, $\omega^2 = 0.19$. Estimations of d' did not differ by warning device, $F(7, 7) = 1.3$, $p > 0.05$.

**Table 11.  Increasing Sight Lines.  Estimates of d' and β.**

**(a) Sight Lines – d'**

| Warning Device | 1986 | 2007 |
|---|---|---|
| No Signs or Signals | 8.03 | 8.06 |
| Other Signs or Signals | 7.59 | 7.58 |
| Crossbucks | 7.70 | 7.93 |
| Stop Signs | 7.06 | 8.07 |
| Special Active Warning Devices | 7.86 | 7.92 |
| Highway Traffic Signals, Wigwags, Bells, or Other Activated Warning Devices | 7.31 | 7.69 |
| Flashing Lights | 7.59 | 7.83 |
| Gates | 7.52 | 7.72 |
| AVERAGE | 7.58 | 7.85 |

**(b) Sight Lights – β**

| Warning Device | 1986 | 2007 |
|---|---|---|
| No Signs or Signals | 0.126 | 0.007 |
| Other Signs or Signals | 0.100 | 0.008 |
| Crossbucks | 0.069 | 0.001 |
| Stop Signs | 0.829 | 0.001 |
| Special Active Warning Devices | 0.002 | 1.49E-04 |
| Highway Traffic Signals, Wigwags, Bells, or Other Activated Warning Devices | 0.012 | 1.38E-04 |
| Flashing Lights | 0.001 | 1.77E-05 |
| Gates | 4.149E-05 | 1.009E-06 |
| AVERAGE | 0.142 | 0.002 |

Although clearing sight lines had a smaller impact on estimations of d' than expected, estimations of β improved in the same time period, from 0.142 in 1986 to 0.002 in 2007; an ANOVA comparing ln β in 1986 to that in 2007 indicated that this shift was statistically reliable, $F(1, 7) = 52.85$, $p < 0.05$, $\omega^2 = 0.28$. Estimations of ln β also differed by warning device, $F(7, 7) = 17.59$, $p < 0.05$, $\omega^2 = 0.63$.  Three groups of warning devices with similar means were identified, and the pattern of results suggest that drivers were more inclined to stop at grade crossings protected by gates or flashing lights than at crossings protected by any of the six other warning devices.  The largest change was at grade crossings protected by stop signs and the smallest change was at grade crossings with gates.

### 4.2.5  Warning Device Reliability

The Highway-Rail Grade Crossing Accident/Incident database recorded 26 total accidents in 1986 attributable to warning device malfunctions and 54 accidents in 2007.  (Appendix B provides details on the number of accidents for each warning device.)  However, FRA modified its reporting structure regarding this safety factor in 1997, so the apparent rise in the number of accidents is the result of additional criteria collected to judge warning device reliability.  In 1986, FRA collected information on warning device reliability using only two criteria:  that a warning device provided the minimum 20-second warning, or that no warning was given.  In 1997, FRA changed the reporting structure, so in 2007, warning device reliability was measured using seven criteria:

1. The warning device provided the minimum 20-second warning.

2. The warning device had an alleged warning time greater than 60 seconds.

3. The warning device had an alleged warning time less than 20 seconds.

4. The warning device allegedly presented no warning.

5. The warning device had a confirmed warning time greater than 60 seconds.

6. The warning device had a confirmed warning time less than 20 seconds.

7. The warning device presented no warning (confirmed).

Thus, five more criteria were used to characterize warning device malfunctions in 2007 compared to 1986 (numbers 2, 3, 5, 6, 7 in the list above), and as a result, more accidents were identified. In fact, an examination of the 2007 data using the 1986 criteria identified only one accident (at a gated crossing).

Given the inconsistency in the information collected on warning device reliability between 1986 and 2007, we were concerned that comparing the two years would be misleading. We chose instead to compare the 2007 data to information collected in 1997 (the first year in which the new criteria were used). Table 12 presents the estimates for d' and β using accidents attributable to warning device reliability. Note that this analysis included only the four active warning devices: special active warning devices; highway traffic signals, wigwags, bells, or other activated warning device; flashing lights; and gates[6]. One swap was needed to calculate the estimates. There were no accidents at grade crossings protected by special active warning devices in either year, so one accident was borrowed from flashing lights and loaned to that category. The cells swapped are highlighted in orange. The results of paired comparisons for the four warning devices are shown in the first set of columns in each table; cells that are shaded in the same color indicate means that are not reliably different.

As the table shows, estimations of d' increased slightly from 1997 (7.61) to 2007 (7.74), but this change was not statistically reliable, $F(1, 3) = 2.19$, $p > 0.05$. The effect of warning device on d' was statistically reliable, however, $F(3, 3) = 11.81$, $p < 0.05$, $\omega^2 = 0.78$. Paired comparisons suggest that crossings protected with special active warning devices had a higher sensitivity than the other active warning devices.

We expected that improvements in warning device reliability would be observed in terms of β, since shorter waiting times or fewer false alarms were expected to encourage drivers to stop. Estimations of β indicate that this was the case, as β dropped by an order of magnitude from 0.001 in 1997 to 0.0001 in 2007 [ln β: $F(1, 3) = 12.16$, $p < 0.05$, $\omega^2 = 0.19$ ]. A statistically reliable main effect of warning device was also present [ln β: $F(3, 3) = 14.5$, $p < 0.05$, $\omega^2 = 0.68$], with the most conservative behavior exhibited at crossings protected by gates and the riskiest behavior at crossings with highway traffic signals, wigwags, bells, or other activated warning devices.

---

[6] The Highway-Rail Accident/Incident database contains records of accidents citing warning device malfunctions for passive warning devices. In 1997, two were noted: one for the crossbuck and one for the stop sign. In 2007, only one was recorded at a crossbuck-protected crossing. All three accidents cited a warning time greater than 60 seconds.

**Table 12. Warning Device Reliability. Estimates of d' and β.**

**(a) Warning Device Reliability – d'**

| Warning Device | 1997 | 2007 |
|---|---|---|
| Special Active Warning Devices | 8.18 | 8.05 |
| Highway Traffic Signals, Wigwags, Bells, or Other Activated Warning Devices | 7.33 | 7.56 |
| Flashing Lights | 7.55 | 7.83 |
| Gates | 7.36 | 7.53 |
| AVERAGE | 7.61 | 7.74 |

**(b) Warning Device Reliability – β**

| Warning Device | 1997 | 2007 |
|---|---|---|
| Special Active Warning Devices | 9.87E-05 | 7.61E-05 |
| Highway Traffic Signals, Wigwags, Bells, or Other Activated Warning Devices | 2.45E-03 | 2.70E-04 |
| Flashing Lights | 1.99E-04 | 1.77E-05 |
| Gates | 2.24E-05 | 2.929E-06 |
| AVERAGE | 0.001 | 9.16E-05 |

### 4.2.6 Summary

Table 13 provides a summary of the safety factors examined in this section. The table shows the changes in d' and β between 1986, when the safety factors were not in effect, and 2007, when they were in use. The two-way ANOVAs that were performed to examine the statistical reliability of the changes in d' and ln β accruing to the introduction of the safety factor and the grade crossing device type (collectively called grade crossing safety) also reported the proportion of variance accounted for ($\omega^2$) by the safety factor and the device type, as shown in Table 13. Overall, mean d' changed by 3.2 percent as a result of introducing the safety factors, while mean β changed by 165 percent. Both changes are statistically reliable (for d', $t(4) = 7.04$, $p < 0.01$; for ln β, $t(4) = 10.27$, $p < 0.01$).

**Table 13. Statistical Summary of the Successful Safety Factors**

| | d' | | | | β | | | |
|---|---|---|---|---|---|---|---|---|
| | | | $\omega2$ | | | | $\omega2$ | |
| Safety Factor | 1986 | 2007 | Safety Factor | Device | 1986 | 2007 | Safety Factor | Device |
| CMV Driver Safety | 7.23 | 7.52 | 0.24 | 0.53 | 0.562 | 0.008 | 0.3 | 0.68 |
| Alerting Lights | 7.23 | 7.54 | 0.25 | 0.54 | 0.507 | 0.006 | 0.34 | 0.63 |
| Reflectorization | 7.47 | 7.66 | 0 | 0.53 | 0.188 | 0.003 | 0.29 | 0.64 |
| Sight Lines | 7.58 | 7.85 | 0.19 | 0 | 0.142 | 0.002 | 0.28 | 0.63 |
| Warning Reliability | 7.61 | 7.74 | 0 | 0.78 | 0.001 | 0.0000916 | 0.19 | 0.68 |
| Average | 7.424 | 7.662 | 0.136 | 0.476 | 0.28 | 0.0038183 | 0.28 | 0.652 |

While the analyses presented in this section suggest that ln β played a much larger role in enhancing safety through the introduction of the safety factors, it is difficult to directly compare d' and ln β because the estimates of d' range from a minimum of zero to infinity (i.e., $0 \leq d' \leq \infty$), but the estimates of ln β can range from negative infinity to positive infinity (i.e., $-\infty \leq \ln \beta \leq \infty$). The use of $\omega^2$ to indirectly compare d' and ln β can avoid this problem because $\omega^2$ indicates the strength of the association between a dependent variable (d' or ln β) and an independent variable (a safety factor) in a unit-less metric (Hays, 1963, p. 325).

A two-way nonparametric ANOVA was performed on the $\omega^2$ data in Table 12 to determine if the differences in strength of association between d' and ln β, between safety factors and device types, and their interaction were reliable (see Bradley, 1968). The mean $\omega^2$ for d' is 0.306, while for ln β it is 0.466. The difference in $\omega^2$ between d' and ln β is statistically reliable (Wilcoxon Signed Rank Test, p =0.0313), indicating that the association between bias and grade crossing safety was 50 percent greater than that for d'. In other words, the overall improvement in safety was due to both increases in ability to detect a train and a bias to stop, but a bias to stop was 50 percent more important.

The mean $\omega^2$ is 0.208 for safety factor and 0.564 for device type. The difference in $\omega^2$ is statistically reliable (Wilcoxon Signed Rank Test, p =0.0313), indicating that the association between device type and grade crossing safety was 1.7 times greater than that for safety factor. That is, the overall improvement in safety was due to both grade crossing devices and safety factors, but grade crossing devices were nearly twice as effective.

Figure 9 shows the values of $\omega^2$ for d' and β as a function of grade crossing safety. It is clear that the interaction term is not reliable in the statistical analysis (Wilcoxon Signed Rank Test, p =0.0625).

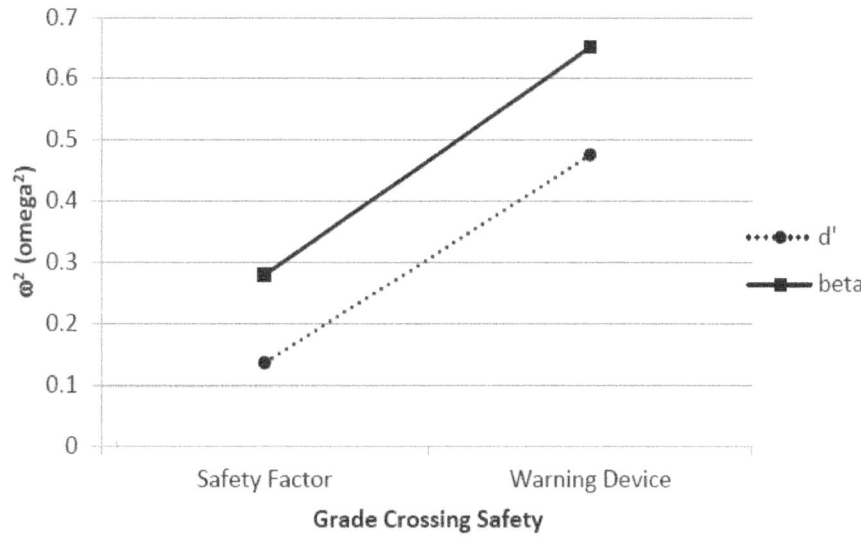

**Figure 9. Proportion of Variance Accounted for as a Function of SDT Metric (d' versus β) and Grade Crossing Safety (Safety Factor versus Device Type)**

This analysis comparing $\omega^2$ revealed some important facts about improving safety at grade crossings. Grade crossing devices, in particular active warning devices, are the most important safety tool because of their ability to increase the bias to stop. This bias to stop is more important than improving the driver's ability to detect the train, and even measures to improve train detection improve driver's bias to stop.

The findings from our analysis differ from those reported by Horton, et al. (2008) who evaluated the impact of these safety factors as a function of the change in the number of accidents (see Tables 7 and 14). Table 14 shows a comparison of the estimates by Horton et al. and the mean $\omega^2$ values calculated in the analysis reported here (across SDT metric).

**Table 14. Comparison of Safety Factors between Horton et al. (% Accident Reduction) and This Report (% Variance Accounted For)**

| Safety Factor | Accident Reduction (%) | Mean ω2 x 100 (%) |
|---|---|---|
| CMV Driver Safety | 34.6 | 27 |
| Alerting Lights | 13.6 | 29.5 |
| Sight Lines | 3.6 | 23.5 |
| Warning Reliability | 3.1 | 9.5 |

As Table 14 shows, Horton, et al. found that between 1994 to 2003, improving CMV driver safety accounted for the largest benefits in grade crossing safety, followed by increasing locomotive conspicuity through the use of alerting lights. Clearing sight lines and improving warning device reliability had more moderate benefits. The use of reflectors was not included in their analysis. Examination of the mean $\omega^2$ values for each safety factor shows a different pattern across a larger timeframe, however, and indicates that CMV driver safety, alerting lights, and sight lines were nearly equivalent in their effect on grade crossing safety. Warning reliability, which only applies to active warning devices and only for the period 1997 to 2007, was much less effective than the other factors in terms of the $\omega^2$ metric, but more effective than indicated by the Horton et al. study. The differences in findings between these two studies therefore raise questions concerning the approach to analysis. We believe that SDT may provide a better framework because changes in accident frequency can be misleading; accidents are rare events and, consequently, are often statistically described using the Poisson probability law, as used here. This issue is discussed in more detail in Section 6.

# 5.    Ideal Observer

Ideal observers hypothesize how real observers process information from their environment and use it to detect signals in noise and make decisions. Ideal observers use all the information available to reach a decision; therefore, the theory of the ideal observer can be used to develop a model of optimal performance and provide hypotheses about how driver behavior can be enhanced to prevent accidents. In this grade crossing application, we are hypothesizing that the real observer uses subjective estimates of the arrival time of his/her highway vehicle and of the train at the grade crossing to make decisions about stopping or proceeding through the grade crossing. Visual search for and localization of the train consumes time during which a decision to stop can be made safely and directly affects accident probability. There can be multiple ideal observers for a particular situation, so comparing the performance between real and ideal observers can allow the mechanisms of detection and decisionmaking to be understood.

Behavior of the ideal observer is described in the context of a simple, heuristic, information processing model of time perception (Raslear et al., 1993). This model assumes an internal pacemaker or clock, which produces a mean rate of output (ticks/unit time) and an associated variance (variability in clock rate across observation periods). Clock variance can arise from a variety of sources inherent in the pacemaker or contributed by other functional elements of the model such as memory and attention, as indicated below. Figure 10 presents the model schematically.

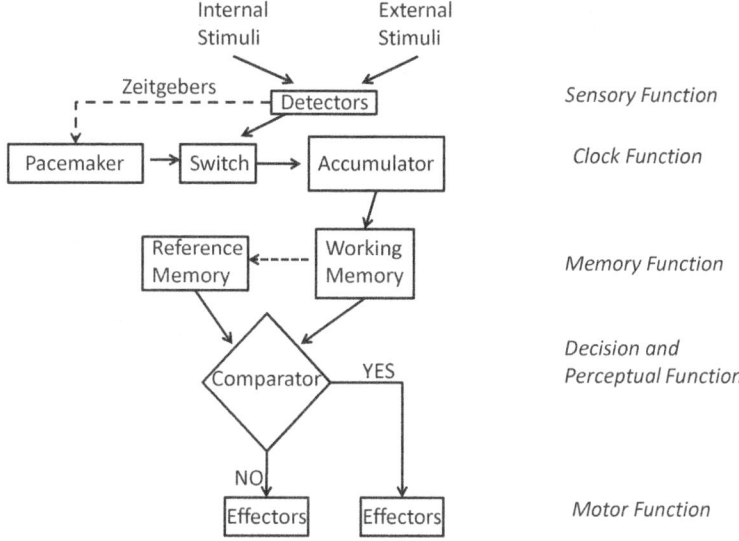

**Figure 10.  Heuristic Information Processing Model of Time Perception**

In the model, two stimulus durations, $T_S$ and $T_N$, are discriminated in the following fashion. The pacemaker (suprachiasmatic nucleus in the hypothalamus. See Rusak and Zucker, 1979) continually produces ticks at some rate that varies over time. When a stimulus is turned on, the ticks are gated by a switch to an accumulator that sums the ticks. The switch has a latency to close and open, thereby mimicking the commonly observed phenomenon of attention. Because of this inherent variability in the switch, gating of ticks to the accumulator does not precisely follow the onset and offset of the stimulus. As a result, the accumulator sum is an inaccurate indicant of stimulus duration. The accumulator sum is stored in memory where it can be compared with a reference value or criterion. The reference value depends on the success of the observer in making correct decisions and is adjusted accordingly. Both the memory of the accumulator sum and the reference value are imperfect, thereby further increasing the variance of the system. Decisions are based on the comparison of the memory of the accumulator sum

33

and the reference value by a decision rule. A common decision rule, and the one assumed here, is that decisions are made to maximize expected value of the decision outcomes.

Sensitivity was previously defined in equation (1). An alternative expression is

$$d' = \frac{\mu_s - \mu_n}{\sigma}, \tag{9}$$

where $\mu_s$ and $\mu_n$ are the means of the signal and noise distributions and $\sigma$ is their common standard deviation. $T_s$ and $T_n$ are stimuli from these distributions. Parameters associated with switch and memory functions are considered to change the denominator of the function defining d' because these functions are assumed to increase variance. Therefore, switch and memory processes act to decrease d'. Switch variance ($\delta$) is usually assumed to be a constant, independent of the durations judged, which is added to the total variance (see Church and Meck, 1984):

$$d' = \frac{\mu_s - \mu_n}{\sqrt{\sigma^2 + \delta}}. \tag{10}$$

Memory variance ($\omega$), on the other hand, is assumed to be a function of the duration judged (Creelman, 1962). So a generic ideal observer with both memory and switch functions would be expressed as

$$d' = \frac{1}{\sqrt{\omega}} \frac{\mu_s - \mu_n}{\sqrt{\sigma^2 + \delta}} \tag{11}$$

Similarly, bias was previously defined in equation (2), but can be alternatively expressed as

$$\beta = \frac{V(CC) + V(FS)}{V(VS) + V(AC)} \times \frac{P(n)}{P(s)}, \tag{12}$$

where $V(CC)$, $V(FS)$, $V(VS)$, $V(AC)$ define the values associated with a payoff matrix that reflects the driver's motivation with respect to correct crossings, false stops, valid stops, and accidents, respectively. In this equation, if the decision is to maximize expected value, the ideal observer would always say "yes" (or would stop) when the value of $\beta < 1$, and would always say "no" (or would cross) when the value of $\beta > 1$. Memory and attention are generally thought to affect both sensitivity and bias (see MacMillan and Creelman, 2005; Swets, 1996), but the effects of these processes on bias have not been extensively discussed in the literature. Bias can be described as a ratio of expected values of the decision outcomes associated with noise and stimulus. In economics, values are theorized to decay with time. The concepts of present value and future value, for instance, make use of the notion that the present value of a good is reduced the further it is realized in the future. As an approximation, we suggest that the time delays associated with $T_s$ and $T_n$ affect bias through the exponential decay function,

$$ke^{(-\lambda T)}, \tag{13}$$

where $\lambda$ is the decay rate and $k$ is a constant. Thus, the generic ideal observer's bias would be

$$\beta = k \exp(-\lambda T) \times \frac{V(CC) + V(FS)}{V(VS) + V(AC)} \times \frac{P(n)}{P(s)}. \tag{14}$$

We were interested in comparing the SDT estimates of driver detection and decisionmaking at grade crossings for each countermeasure discussed in Section 4 to the performance of an *ideal observer*. To conduct this analysis of the ideal observer, we considered the 1986 estimates for d' and $\beta$ and developed methods to predict the changes in d' and $\beta$ for the ideal observer. Many of the methods rely on basic human factors perception data as reported in the literature. Section 5.1 considers changes in sensitivity, and Section 5.2 considers changes in bias.

## 5.1 Sensitivity for the Ideal Observer

Our model of the ideal observer hypothesizes that drivers use subjective estimates of motor vehicle and train arrival times at the grade crossing to make decisions to stop or proceed. The ideal observer's sensitivity reflects his/her perception of the time available to cross the grade crossing, $T_c^*$, versus the amount of time to stop, $T_s^*$.

To estimate $T_c^*$ and $T_s^*$, it is necessary to understand the relative location of the highway vehicle and train with respect to the grade crossing. Two sight distances allow the driver to determine $T_c^*$ and $T_s^*$. One is the sight distance along the highway measured from the driver to the nearest rail ($d_H$). This is the distance where the vehicle could be stopped safely without encroaching upon the grade crossing. $d_H$ can be calculated as follows (Ogden, 2007):

$$d_H = AV_v t + \frac{BV_v^2}{a} + D + d_e,$$ (15)

where

> $A$ = constant = 1.47, $B$ = constant = 1.075, $V_v$ = vehicle velocity (mph);
> $t$ = perception-reaction time (s); this is assumed to be 2.5 s;
> $a$ = deceleration rate; assumed to be 11.2 feet per second$^2$ (ft/s$^2$);
> $D$ = distance from the front of the vehicle or the stop line to the nearest rail, assumed to be 15 ft;
> $d_e$ = distance from the driver to the front of the vehicle, assumed to be 8 ft.

The other sight distance reflects the distance to and along the railroad tracks on which the train may be approaching the grade crossing from either direction. ($d_T$). $d_T$ can be calculated as

$$d_T = \frac{V_T}{V_V}(A)V_v t + \frac{BV_v^2}{a} + 2D + L + W,$$ (16)

where

> $V_v$ = vehicle velocity (mph);
> $t$ = perception-reaction time (s); this is assumed to be 2.5 s;
> $a$ = deceleration rate; assumed to be 11.2 ft/s$^2$;
> $D$ = distance from the front of the vehicle or the stop line to the nearest rail, assumed to be 15 ft;
> $L$ = vehicle length, assumed to be 65 ft; and
> $W$ = distance between the outer rails (5 ft for a single track).

Current vehicle position ($d_H$) and the current train position ($d_T$) combined with information about the relative velocities of the vehicle and the train can be used to calculate the *actual* time required to proceed through the grade crossing (denoted as $T_c$) and the *actual* time needed to stop (denoted as $T_s$).

For instance, if a driver is approaching a grade crossing at 30 mph, and a train is approaching that same crossing at a velocity of 10 mph, $d_H$ equals 219.63 ft and $d_T$ equals 98.88 ft (see also Table 32 in Ogden, 2007). From these values, the time to cross, $T_c$, or the time to stop, $T_s$, can be calculated as distance divided by velocity. That is

$$T_c = d_T / V_T = 6.74 \text{ s,}$$ (17)

and

$$T_s = d_H / V_v = 4.99 \text{s,}$$ (18)

where $V_T$ and $V_v$ reflect the velocities of the train (14.67 ft/s) and vehicle (44 ft/s), respectively.

Note that $T_c$ and $T_s$ reflect the *actual* time to cross or stop. However, human perception of time is not the same as actual or physical time. It is typically found in the human time perception literature that short durations are overestimated and long durations are underestimated. A study of time to passage of a moving object by Kaiser and Mowafy (1993, see Figs. 7 and 8) allows the relationship between the perceived time to a crossing (T*) and the actual time to crossing (T) to be defined as

$$T* = 0.84375\ T + 0.84375. \tag{19}$$

As noted previously in equation (9), in SDT, sensitivity or d' is defined as the difference between the means of the signal ($\mu_s$) and noise ($\mu_n$) distributions divided by their common standard deviation ($\sigma$):

$$d' = \frac{\mu_s - \mu_n}{\sigma}$$

If the distributions of signal and noise are Gaussian, $\sigma$ is independent of the means and must be estimated. However, a widely applied theory of time discrimination (Gibbon, 1977), Scalar Expectancy Theory (SET), assumes that physical durations generate distributions of time estimates which have well-defined statistical characteristics. In particular, SET assumes that the mean and the standard deviation of the distribution are proportional to the interval being timed (T), so that the coefficient of variation is a constant:

$$\text{Mean} = \mu T, \tag{20}$$

$$\text{Standard Deviation} = \sigma T, \tag{21}$$

$$\text{Coefficient of Variation} = \gamma = \mu/\sigma. \tag{22}$$

Using the assumptions of SET concerning the distribution of time estimates, it is fairly easy to derive a measure of sensitivity for a discrimination between $T_c^*$ and $T_s^*$:

$$d' = \gamma \frac{1}{\sqrt{\omega}} \frac{\left| T_c^* - T_s^* \right|}{\sqrt{(T_c^* + (T_c^* - T_s^*))^2 + (T_c^*)^2 + \delta}}, \tag{23}$$

where $\gamma = \mu/\sigma = 57.47$ and $\delta = 5.21$. For the purposes of this analysis, we estimate the value $\gamma$ as 57.47, as used in Raslear (1996). This value was based on a study conducted by Bootsma and Oudejans (1993, experiment 1) on perceived time to collision. The value of $\delta$ is based on Creelman (1962). There are no estimates of $\omega$ in the literature that seem reasonable for time discriminations at grade crossings. Since the overall effect of memory variance is to decrease the value of d' with time, we use the same exponential time decay function suggested for bias (see equation (11) above). However, in the case of sensitivity, the decay function depends on real time ($T_c$ and $T_s$ rather than $T_c^*$ and $T_s^*$). This is because memory decays in real time, but perceived economic (subjective) value decays in perceived time. So we rewrite equation 23 as

$$d' = \gamma \bullet k \exp(-\lambda T_c) \frac{\left| T_c^* - T_s^* \right|}{\sqrt{(T_c^* + (T_c^* - T_s^*))^2 + (T_c^*)^2 + \delta}}. \tag{24}$$

For this analysis, we estimated $T_c^*$ and $T_s^*$ as a function of the anticipated benefits of several of the different countermeasures combined. This was done for practical reasons: with the exception of the CMV safety rules and improvements in grade crossing device reliability, the other countermeasures all involve improvements in detection through visual search. Train horns, which are not considered a countermeasure because train horns were already in use in 1986, also serve this function as was noted by Raslear (1996). Consequently, we develop the ideal observer from a baseline model in which visual search for the train is aided by the train horn (this baseline model is presented in Section 5.1.1). This section naturally includes a discussion of sight line improvements through the removal of visual clutter at the grade crossing. The addition of alerting lights and reflectorization of rail cars further reduce visual search time and improve train detection in the final model of the ideal observer; their combined effects

36

are considered in Section 5.1.2. Finally, we conclude this section with an examination of how sensitivity of the ideal observer may be influenced by CMV driver safety rules (Section 5.1.3) and warning device reliability (Section 5.1.4).

## 5.1.1 *Visual Search Baseline*

We assume that a driver is approaching the grade crossing at a speed of 30 mph, and that a train is approaching at 10 mph. The driver must scan a visual field of approximately 180 degrees, and the time required to search this field (to detect the train, for example) increases as the number of items in the visual field increases. Additionally, visual search in the real world does not necessarily progress in a linear fashion. The target item may be found after examining a couple of items or sometimes requires a thorough search of the entire environment. Raslear (1996) referenced the work of Luce (1986) to estimate the impact of clutter on visual search. An estimate of the average time to search for a target can be derived from the following formula:

$$S = \frac{1}{2}kM + r_0, \tag{25}$$

where $k$ = mean time required to search an item, $M$ = the number of items, and $r_0$ = residual time.

The variance in the visual search can be described by

$$\eta^2 = \eta_m^2 M + \eta_r^2, \tag{26}$$

where $\eta_m^2$ = per item variance, and $\eta_r^2$ = residual variance.

Raslear (1996) estimated the parameters using data from the human factors literature as follows:

$k = 0.02$ (Sternberg, 1966), $r_0 = 0.4$ (Sternberg, 1966), $\eta_m^2 M = M^2/12$, and $\eta_r^2 = 8.2944$ (Luce, 1986). Raslear (1996) then modeled the effect of visual clutter by adjusting the values for the perceived time to cross taking into account greater sight lines and the perceived time to stop by the value of $S$ and accounting for the variance, $\sigma$, in the calculation of d'.

Visual search at the grade crossing may be aided by the sound of the train horn. As noted previously, the driver must scan a visual field of approximately 180 degrees. However, data regarding sound localization indicates that pure tones can be localized with only a 10-degree error. Therefore, we assume here that the sound from a train horn reduces this search field to 10 degrees (i.e., one-eighteenth of the size). This reduces S which affects the perceived times to cross and to stop. It also reduces the variance due to visual search by a factor of 18.

$T_c = 6.74$ and $T_s = 4.99$ as noted above. These values are reduced by S, accounting for visual search given a number of items of clutter, aided by a train horn; so,

$$T_c = 6.74 - (S/18), \tag{27}$$

and

$$T_s = 4.99 - (S/18) \tag{28}$$

as shown in Table 15. The perceived times to cross and stop were then calculated as shown in the table.

**Table 15. Baseline Ideal Observer with Visual Search and Train Horn**

| Number of Items | $T_c$ | $T_s$ | $T_c^*$ | $T_s^*$ | d' |
|---|---|---|---|---|---|
| 0 | 6.34 | 4.59 | 6.1932 | 4.717 | 7.48 |
| 1 | 6.3395 | 4.5899 | 6.1927 | 4.7165 | 7.48 |
| 2 | 6.339 | 4.589 | 6.1923 | 4.7161 | 7.48 |
| 4 | 6.338 | 4.588 | 6.1914 | 4.7152 | 7.48 |
| 8 | 6.336 | 4.586 | 6.1895 | 4.7133 | 7.47 |
| 16 | 6.331 | 4.582 | 6.1858 | 4.7096 | 7.45 |
| 32 | 6.32 | 4.573 | 6.1784 | 4.7022 | 7.33 |
| 61 | 6.31 | 4.56 | 6.16 | 4.69 | 6.95 |

Sensitivity can then be calculated using the following formula:

$$d' = \gamma \bullet k \exp(-\lambda T_c) \frac{\left| T_c^* - T_s^* \right|}{\sqrt{(T_c^* + (T_c^* - T_s^*))^2 + (T_c^*)^2 + \frac{\eta^2}{18} + \delta}}. \tag{29}$$

where k is 0.9, λ is 0.001, δ is 5.21, and γ is 57.47. The other variables' values depend on the amount of visual clutter.

Therefore, in this baseline model, it can be seen that increasing visual clutter decreases sensitivity (d') when the amount of clutter reaches a critical level of eight or more items. In 1986, the average d' was 6.95, which according to this baseline model would require, on average, 61 items of visual clutter.

### 5.1.2 Alerting Lights and Reflectors

To quantify the potential benefit of alerting lights, we relied on the results of a study by Carroll, Multer, and Markos (1995), which compared the distances at which trains could be detected when equipped with different visual alerting devices. In the study, participants were seated at a "simulated" grade crossing (the grade crossing was located at a railroad yard, so there was little to no train or other vehicular traffic). Participants' primary task was to perform a visual monitoring task that simulated the attentional demands imposed by driving. Participants then indicated when they first detected a train equipped with one of the alerting devices. Among these visual alerting devices were the standard headlight alone and crossing lights.

Carroll, et al. (1995) reported that trains equipped with crossing lights could be detected from a distance of 464 m (1,548 ft) and the standard headlight alone was detected from a distance of 377 m (1,257 ft). These distances can be converted to estimate the amount of time that a train can be detected before it arrives at the crossing. Carroll, et al. estimated that for a train travelling 25 mph, a train with crossing lights can be detected 42.2 seconds before its arrival, whereas a train with headlight alone can be detected 34.3 seconds before arriving at the crossing. In other words, the data shows an overall 23 percent benefit provided for the use of the crossing lights over the headlight alone.

Therefore, to capture the benefits of alerting lights, we increased $T_c$ and $T_s$ by 23 percent in the baseline model.

We can conduct a similar analysis to quantify the impact of reflectors. The detection distance at which trains can be seen at the grade crossing as a function of reflectors is derived from data collected by Multer, Conti, and Sheridan (2001). In that study, Multer, et al. (2001) asked participants to drive a test

38

course in a simulator and identify each object in the scene. The test course contained highway intersections and grade crossings, and one of the objects to be identified were trains with and without reflectors. The results indicated that trains with reflectors were detected at almost three times the distance of trains without reflectors (1,113 ft for reflectorized trains, 373.5 ft for trains without reflectors). Thus, the benefits of reflectors are estimated here to improve detection distance 2.97 times that for trains without reflectors.

Observing the benefits of reflectors may be limited by the implementation rate, however. The use of reflectors has been phased in since the final rule recommending their use was published in 2005(see *Reflectorization of Rail Freight Rolling Stock; Final Rule* for more information), so not all trains had reflectors in 2007. For the purposes of calculating an estimate for the ideal observer, we assume that this implementation rate is 60 percent.

Therefore, combining the effect of alerting lights and reflectors, $T_{s+}$ can be calculated as follows:

$$T_{s+} = (T_s \times 1.23 \times 2.97 \times 0.6) - (S/18). \tag{30}$$

With regard to calculating $T_{c+}$, we considered that the benefit of reflectors is primarily in reducing accidents in which a driver runs into the train (RIT). In other words, the sight distance along the railroad tracks on which the train may be approaching the grade crossing is not expected to increase, since the impact of reflectors is expected when the train is *at* the crossing. Therefore,

$$T_{c+} = (T_c \times 1.23) - (S/18). \tag{31}$$

Sensitivity is then calculated as

$$d' = \gamma \bullet k \exp(-\lambda T_{c+}) \frac{\left| T_{c+}^* - T_{s+}^* \right|}{\sqrt{(T_{c+}^* + (T_{c+}^* - T_{s+}^*))^2 + (T_{c+}^*)^2 + \frac{\eta^2}{18} + \delta}}. \tag{32}$$

Here k is 0.9, $\lambda$ is 0.001, $\delta$ is 5.21, and $\gamma$ is 57.47. The other variables' values depend on the amount of visual clutter. Table 16 shows the main results.

**Table 16. Ideal Observer Enhanced from Baseline with Alerting Lights and Reflectors**

| Number of Items | $T_{c+}$ | $T_{s+}$ | $T_{c+}^*$ | $T_{s+}^*$ | d' |
|---|---|---|---|---|---|
| 0 | 7.89 | 10.5386 | 7.5012 | 9.7357 | 12.11 |
| 1 | 7.8898 | 10.538 | 7.5008 | 9.7352 | 12.11 |
| 2 | 7.8893 | 10.5375 | 7.5003 | 9.7347 | 12.11 |
| 4 | 7.8882 | 10.5364 | 7.4994 | 9.7338 | 12.11 |
| 8 | 7.886 | 10.5342 | 7.4975 | 9.732 | 12.09 |
| 16 | 7.8816 | 10.5298 | 7.4938 | 9.7283 | 12.04 |
| 32 | 7.8728 | 10.521 | 7.4864 | 9.7208 | 11.82 |
| 61 | 7.8568 | 10.505 | 7.4729 | 9.7074 | 11.22 |

From Table 16, we see that adding alerting lights and reflectors increases d' for 61 items of clutter from 6.95 in the baseline model to 11.22. Improving sight lines until there are only 4 items left at the grade crossing, further increases d' to 12.11. The average sensitivity for 2007 was 7.24.

### 5.1.3  CMV Driver Safety Rules

Unlike train horns, alerting lights, sight lines and reflectors, CMV rules do not simply affect visual search times and variance, the CMV rules change driver behavior.  The rules require commercial drivers to stop at all crossings, thereby (hopefully) forcing direct visual search in both directions on the track from the point of the grade crossing.  Therefore, the decision faced by the commercial motor vehicle driver is not whether to stop or cross, it is whether to cross following a stop.  That is, in developing an estimate of sensitivity for the ideal observer, we need to consider only train speed because the highway vehicle speed is zero.

In this example, train speed is 10 mph (14.67 ft/s), $T_c$ = 16.36 s, which is the amount of time necessary for the highway vehicle to just clear the tracks from a stop; it is also enough time for the train to reach the grade crossing (see Ogden, 2007, p. 68 for formula for vehicle stopped at a crossing).  Adjusting for alerting lights and visual search with four items of visual clutter, $T_{c+}$ = 19.72 s and $T_{C+}^*$ = 17.48 s, computing sensitivity with $T_{s+}^*$ = 0, d' > 22.  However, if we assume that commercial drivers perform a "rolling stop" at the grade crossing instead of a full stop, we can subtract the time to put the vehicle into gear and the perception reaction time from the time necessary to clear the tracks.  This sets $T_{s+}$ to 14.36 s, $T_{s+}^*$ = 12.96 s, and d' = 8.13.  Since the observed value of d' for CMV rules in 2007 was 7.52, the "rolling stop" scenario is reasonable.

### 5.1.4  Warning Device Reliability

Gil, Multer, and Yeh (2009) demonstrated in an experiment that increasing grade crossing warning device reliability by increasing warning positive predictive value increases sensitivity.  Rice and McCarley (2011) found similar results in a simulated x-ray baggage screening task; false alarms decreased sensitivity and reduced use in an automated aid.  Reliability is a serious problem when a warning device fails to activate.  Horton, et al. (2009) indicates that the rate of activation failures in 1992 was 3.851 percent and was reduced to 0.745 percent in 2003, a 3.106 percent change.  Data from 1997 and 2007 indicate that d' increased over that period of time from 7.61 to 7.74, a 1.71 percent change (see Section 4.2.5).  Thus, experimental and field observations agree.

Motorist behavior may also be changed by device reliability, in a way similar to that in the CMV situation.  Motorists who experience a device activation failure may now proceed with greater caution at all grade crossings with active devices.  They may, in fact, mimic the CMV driver who proceeds to cross after a rolling stop.  The difference is that CMV drivers exhibit this behavior at *all* grade crossings, but other, exposed motorists would only do this at active crossings.  According to FRA data, in 2007 47.73 percent of grade crossings were equipped with active devices.  If 0.745 percent of devices at those crossings failed to activate, exposure would be 0.3556 percent.  A weighted average (based on exposure to warning device failure) of $T_c$, $T_c^*$ and $T_s^*$ values for CMV and for the combination of train horn, alerting lights, reflectorization, and improved sight lines (four items of visual clutter) allows d' to be calculated for noncommercial motorists, given all of these enhancements, as the following:

$$T_c = 0.003556*6.34 + 0.996444*7.888182 = 7.883, \tag{33}$$

$$T_c^* = 0.003556*17.48 + 0.996444*7.499 = 7.417, \tag{34}$$

$$T_s^* = 0.003556*12.96 + 0.996444*9.7338 = 9.745, \tag{35}$$

and

$$d' = 12.72.$$

This value of d' is higher than the mean for 2007, 7.24.  However, it is expected that an ideal observer performs better than a real observer because the ideal observer uses all the available information to the fullest extent possible.

## 5.2    Bias to Stop (Beta)

As noted in equation (12) above, the generic ideal observer's bias is given by

$$\beta = k \exp(-\lambda T) \times \frac{V(CC) + V(FS)}{V(VS) + V(AC)} \times \frac{P(n)}{P(s)},$$

where  k =0.9, $\lambda$ = 0.001, P(s) is the probability of a train, P(n) = 1-P(s), and *V(CC), V(FS), V(VS), V(AC)* are the values associated with a payoff matrix that reflect the driver's motivation with respect to correct crossings, false stops, valid stops, and accidents, respectively.  The term [V(CC) + V(FS)] is the value of noise (V(n)) whereas [V(VS) + V(AC)] is the value of signal (V(s)).

First, we note that changes in P(s) directly affect bias.  Train traffic doubled from 1986 through 2007 from an average of 4.19 trains per day to 9.15 trains per day.  This increase in train traffic directly influences the probability of a train or signal, P(s), and the probability of no train or noise, P(n).

The calculations to estimate the probability of a train ($p_T$) at a grade crossing were described in detail in Section 2.  Recall from equation (6) that:

$$p_T = 1 - e^{-\lambda_T},$$

where $\lambda_T$ represents the mean frequency of a train at a grade crossing in a 1-min period of time.  $\lambda_T$ is calculated from the train rate per day at a crossing.

In 1986, the overall probability of a train at a grade crossing, P(s), was 0.0029; by 2007, the probability of a train at a grade crossing doubled to 0.0058 (note that the probabilities of a train will differ as a function of the warning device; for simplicity in this discussion, we consider the average probability across all grade crossing warning devices.  As a result of this change, the ratio P(n)/P(s), also called the prior odds, was just a little over two times higher in 1986 (343.73) than in 2007 (170.63).  The change in the *observed* bias for these years was much greater, however; in 1986, we estimated $\beta$ at 1.45 and in 2007, this estimate dropped to 0.02.  Therefore, the change in *observed bias* was on the order of 70 times, suggesting that other factors contributed to the change in bias, and these other factors can be accounted for via the payoff matrix.  In fact, in 2007, we can estimate that the payoff matrix reflecting the motivation to stop is 8531.5 times greater than the motivation to proceed (0.02/170.63).

The use of regulations to improve CMV driver safety and efforts to improve warning device reliability are expected to improve driver decisionmaking by changing bias.  However, the analysis in Section 4.2.1 showed that other efforts, primarily thought to improve train detection, also affected bias.  This section develops an ideal observer for bias for the five safety improvements considered in the previous section.  Train horns are not explicitly considered because they were already in use in 1986.  However, for that reason, bias associated with train horns is accounted for in the baseline for calculations of $\beta$ in 2007 for the ideal observer.  The model is then further developed to consider the impacts of alerting lights, reflectorization, sight line improvement, and warning reliability.

### 5.2.1  CMV Driver Safety Rules

The values associated with the payoff matrix can be estimated for the ideal observer by considering the expected impact of specific countermeasures.  For example, regulations to improve commercial motor vehicle driver safety disqualifies a driver for a period of 60 days (d) up to 1 year if he or she commits a violation(s) at a grade crossing (see 49 CFR Part 383.51).  This regulation was not expected to have a significant economic impact, since the Federal Highway Administration (FHWA) indicated that the majority of motor carriers already instructed their drivers to comply with laws and regulations at highway-rail grade crossings.  The personal economic impact on the driver can be assessed through the payoff matrix.

Consider a driver who commits his/her first violation. According to the regulation, if cited/ticketed, the driver must be disqualified for at least 60 d. The U.S. Department of Labor, Bureau of Labor Statistics provides mean hourly wages for three different classes of commercial motor vehicle drivers (truck drivers, heavy and tractor-trailer ($18.87/h); truck drivers, light or delivery services ($14.96/h); and motor vehicle operators, other ($14.95/h). See http://www.bls.gov/oes/current/oes_nat.htm#53-0000). A general average hourly wage for all truck drivers is approximately $16.26/h. Assume that a commercial motor vehicle driver spends 70 h on duty over 8 consecutive days (with a 34-hour restart period; see 49 CFR Part 395). A 60-day suspension could cost up to $8,531 in lost wages. A second violation within a 3-year period requires a disqualification of at least 120 d—approximately $17,063 in lost wages, and a third violation requires a one-year disqualification—up to $51,930 in lost wages). According to Horton, et al. grade crossing incidents involving commercial drivers accounted for 23.7 percent of all incidents in 2003. Thus, the maximum expected value of a grade crossing incident, based on violations of the CMV rule, would be 0.237 x $51,930. Accordingly, we calculate

$$\beta = 170.63 x 0.9 e^{-0.001 T_c^*} x \left[ \frac{1}{0.237 \times 51930} \right] = 0.0123, \qquad (36)$$

where $T_c^*$ = 17.48, and 170.63 is the prior odds.

The observed value of $\beta$ was 0.008 in 2007 and 0.562 in 1986 for CMV driver safety rules. It is important to note, however, that the subjective cost estimate to stop used for the ideal observer currently captures only lost wages. Other costs associated with the disqualification (such as fines or points added to the driver's personal license) could further reduce bias. Additionally, the values set for the payoff matrix may not be monetary. However, because these costs are subjective, they are not as easily quantified for the ideal observer.

### 5.2.2 Alerting Lights, Reflectors, Sight Lines, and Warning Reliabiltiy

Unfortunately, there are no documented costs and benefits associated with the other safety factors. However, we can derive estimates for costs and benefits using Equation 12. Since we know the value of $\beta_{1986}$ and the prior odds (P(n)/P(s) = 343.73), we can calculate V(n)/V(s) for 1986. Additionally, because $\beta_{1986} < \beta_{2007}$ for all safety factors, it follows that V(s) has increased between 1986 and 2007. To estimate the change in V(s) from 1986 to 2007, we suggest using the funding provided to Operation Lifesaver as a proxy since Operation Lifesaver activities are targeted at biasing motorists to stop, look, and listen at all grade crossings.

The Department of Transportation's funding of Operation Lifesaver started in 1988 with $69,000. In 2007, funding was $1,797,328. Accordingly, we estimate that V(s) has increased 26.05-fold.

Table 17 shows the values of $\beta_{1986}$, $\left(\frac{V(n)}{V(s)}\right)_{1986}$, $\beta_{2007}$, $T_c^*$ for alerting lights, reflectors, sight lines and warning reliability. From these values, we calculated $\hat{\beta}_{2007E}$ for each safety factor using the following equation:

$$\hat{\beta}_{2007E} = 170.63 x 0.9 e^{-0.001 T_c^*} x \left[ \left(\frac{V(n)}{V(s)}\right)_{1986} x \frac{1}{26.05} \right]. \qquad (37)$$

For completeness, the parameters for CMV have been added to the table.

## Table 17. Ideal Observer Estimates of Bias for 2007 ($\hat{\beta}_{2007E}$)

| Safety Factor | $\beta_{1986}$ | $\left(\dfrac{V(n)}{V(s)}\right)_{1986}$ | $\beta_{2007}$ | $T_c^*$ | $\hat{\beta}_{2007E}$ |
|---|---|---|---|---|---|
| Alerting Lights | 0.507 | 0.001475 | 0.006 | 7.84 | 0.0086 |
| Reflectorization | 0.188 | 0.000547 | 0.003 | 6.53 | 0.0032 |
| Sight Lines | 0.142 | 0.000413 | 0.002 | 6.18 | 0.0024 |
| Warning Reliability | 0.001 | 0.00000291 | 0.000092 | 7.42 | 0.00002 |
| CMV | 0.562 | 0.0016345 | 0.008 | 17.48 | 0.0123 |

The correlation between $\hat{\beta}_{2007E}$ and $\beta_{2007}$ is 0.9943 (p < 0.01).

Public education campaigns are sometimes combined with enforcement initiatives to encourage drivers to comply. To understand how such programs influence beta for the ideal observer, we needed to develop an estimate of their impact. Such an estimate can be developed from the results of a joint study conducted by FRA in conjunction with the Illinois Commerce Commission in several Illinois communities (see Illinois Commerce Commission, 2005 and Sposato, Bien-Aime, and Chaudhary, 2006). Residents were exposed to a public education campaign on grade crossing safety, which included public service announcements aired on television and radio, Operator Lifesaver presentations, and rail safety messages in routine mailings and telephone systems, to name a few. Additionally, an enforcement program was conducted which included techniques such as the Officer on the Train programs, routine patrols at the grade crossing with focused enforcement at areas with typically high rates of traffic violations, and positive reinforcement for compliance. Driver behavior at three grade crossings was recorded on videos before, during, and after the program. These videos were then analyzed, and violations were identified and classified into three categories.

- Type 1A: violations in which the flashing lights were activated but the gate arms were up,
- Type IB: violations in which the lights were flashing and the gate arms were descending, and
- Type 2: violations in which the lights were flashing and the gate arms were lowered.

The data for each violation type is shown in Table 18 below.

**Table 18. Violation Rate as Reported in Sposato, et al. (2006). The rate of violations is one unit per train.**

| Violation | Before | During | After | Overall Change |
|---|---|---|---|---|
| Type 1A | 0.46 | 0.48 | 0.53 | +15% |
| Type 1B | 1.40 | 1.10 | 1.00 | -29% |
| Type 2 | 0.78 | 0.36 | 0.22 | -72% |
| Total | 2.64 | 1.94 | 1.75 | -34% |

As Table 18 shows, the data showed an increase in the rate of Type 1A violations, but a drop in the more serious Type 1B and Type 2 violations. Overall, there was a 34 percent drop in violations due to the combined education and enforcement program.

Previously, we estimated that Operation Lifesaver increased V(s) by 26.05. Based on the results of Sposato, et al. (2006), we can assume that V(s) will increase by at least 34 percent when an education campaign is combined with enforcement (i.e., V(s) = 34.91). Therefore, we can calculate $\hat{\beta}_{2007EE}$ for a combined education and enforcement campaign using the following:

$$\hat{\beta}_{2007EE} = 170.63x0.9e^{-0.001T_c^*}x\left[\left(\frac{V(n)}{V(s)}\right)_{1986}x\frac{1}{34.91}\right] \tag{38}$$

Table 19 shows the values of $\beta_{1986}$, $\beta_{2007}$, $\hat{\beta}_{2007E}$, and $\hat{\beta}_{2007EE}$ for alerting lights, reflectors sight lines, and warning reliability.

**Table 19. Ideal Observer Estimates of Bias for Combined Education and Enforcement Programs (2007, $\hat{\beta}_{2007EE}$ )**

| Safety Factor | $\beta_{1986}$ | $\beta_{2007}$ | $\hat{\beta}_{2007E}$ | $\hat{\beta}_{2007EE}$ |
|---|---|---|---|---|
| Alerting Lights | 0.507 | 0.006 | 0.0086 | 0.0064 |
| Reflectorization | 0.188 | 0.003 | 0.0032 | 0.0024 |
| Sight Lines | 0.142 | 0.002 | 0.0024 | 0.0018 |
| Warning Reliability | 0.001 | 0.000092 | 0.00002 | $1.27 \times 10^{-05}$ |

The correlation between $\hat{\beta}_{2007EE}$ and $\beta_{2007}$ is 0.9920 (p < 0.01).

## 5.3 Summary

It is clear from the ideal observer analysis for sensitivity and bias that each of the successful safety factors has a theoretical basis for positively changing both sensitivity and bias, just as the empirical observations in Section 4 demonstrate. The analysis in Section 4 also showed that the bias to stop had a stronger association with grade crossing safety than sensitivity as indicated by $\omega^2$. Therefore, it is of interest to see if there is a similar trend in the ideal observers.

The proportion of variance accounted for, $\omega^2$, can be roughly calculated as described by Hays (1963, p. 325, equation 10.19.2) from the values of d' and ln $\beta$ observed in 1986 and estimated for 2007 from the ideal observer models. The equation for $\omega^2$ is:

$$\omega^2 = \frac{\sigma_Y^2 - \sigma_{Y|X}^2}{\sigma_Y^2}, \tag{39}$$

where $\sigma_Y^2$ is the marginal variance for d' or ln $\beta$ and $\sigma_{Y|X}^2$ is the conditional variance for a safety factor.

Recall that the ideal observer for sensitivity was calculated separately for CMV driver safety, warning reliability, and visual search (the combination of which included alerting lights, reflectorization, and sight lines). Table 20 shows the marginal variance and conditional variance for d' and ln $\beta$ for each of the factors for which an ideal observer was calculated. Table 20 also shows the empirical and ideal observer $\omega^2$ values.

It is clear that the ideal observer $\omega^2$ values are much higher than the empirically obtained values. This is due to the fact that the empirical values were calculated from data that included variance associated with differences in d' and ln $\beta$ for grade crossing devices, but that variance was not included in the ideal observer models because the effect of grade crossing devices was not modeled. Nevertheless, one can see that ln β has a stronger association with safety for both empirical and ideal observers. The correlation of ideal and empirical $\omega^2$ values is 0.8021 (df = 6, p < 0.05), which indicates that the ideal observer models provide a good rank ordering of the safety factors across d' and ln β metrics with regard to safety outcomes.

**Table 20. Empirical and Ideal Observer Comparison of $\omega^2$**

| | d' | | | ln β | | |
| | $\omega^2$ | | | $\omega^2$ | | |
| | $\sigma^2_{Y|X}$ | Empirical | Ideal | $\sigma^2_{Y|X}$ | Empirical | Ideal |
|---|---|---|---|---|---|---|
| **CMV** | 0.2015 | 0.24 | 0.99 | 4.52 | 0.3 | 0.9396 |
| **Visual Search** | 5.48 | 0.15 | 0.74 | | | |
| **Alerting Lights** | | | | 4.92 | 0.34 | 0.9342 |
| **Reflectorization** | | | | 4.28 | 0.29 | 0.9428 |
| **Sight Lines** | | | | 4.54 | 0.28 | 0.9393 |
| **Warning Reliability** | 6.53 | 0 | 0.69 | 1.43 | 0.19 | 0.981 |
| **Mean** | | 0.129 | 0.81 | | 0.28 | 0.947 |
| $\sigma^2_Y$ | 21.26 | | | 74.79 | | |

# 6. Discussion

Highway-rail grade crossing safety has improved dramatically in the past 20 years, a change that is attributable largely to grade crossing closures, the installation and upgrade of active warning devices, and public education efforts. However, further improvement of grade crossing safety requires a better understanding of accident trends and countermeasures to specifically and strategically target problem areas, one of which continues to be risky driver behavior or poor judgment (Office of the Inspector General, 2004). We applied SDT to develop a model for driver decisionmaking at grade crossings because the theory provides a framework for describing decisions at grade crossings with respect to human perception, attitudes, and motivations. Often, these factors are key to understanding the root cause of grade crossing collisions. Although engineering solutions can be effective, their success is often dependent on how drivers perceive their utility (a fact that was reflected in the results of this current analysis).

We conducted empirical and theoretical tests of our model to understand how different warning devices and countermeasures influenced drivers' decisions at grade crossings in the 21 years from 1986 to 2007. The results indicated that drivers became more willing to stop at grade crossings, and this was reflected in a large and statistically reliable shift in response bias ($\beta$). Driver's ability to detect trains at grade crossings was high in 1986, but it also showed a statistically reliable increase through 2007. Warning device effectiveness, derived by comparing the risk of an accident with the observed accident rate, improved as well, primarily because drivers were more willing to stop. The change in motorists' ability to detect a train had little impact on warning device effectiveness, which makes intuitive sense, since the warning devices at the grade crossing are not part of the train and cannot enhance the signal (train) by themselves.

The data shows that ability to detect an approaching train was generally higher at passive grade crossings than active grade crossings, whereas drivers were more inclined to stop at active grade crossings than at passive ones (there were a few exceptions, as will be discussed below). The increased ability to detect a train at passive grade crossings suggests that drivers look more for an approaching train at passive grade crossings than at active grade crossings, possibly because there is no warning device at passive grade crossings to indicate whether a train is approaching. However, the higher bias (willingness to stop) at active grade crossings than at passive grade crossings suggests that drivers are more likely to stop at active grade crossings because they rely on the information provided by the warning device at those locations. In fact, the data shows that drivers had the highest ability to detect a train at crossings with no signs or signals, and crossings with gates were most likely to encourage drivers to stop.

The one exception was driver response to the stop sign at grade crossings; of the eight warning devices, the stop sign was one of the least sensitive (ability to detect a train), but despite the low signal-to-noise ratio, drivers on the whole made the most risky decisions (least willingness to stop). In fact, the stop sign also had one of the lowest device effectiveness ratios (6.60), and this was almost equal to that at grade crossings with no warning device at all. The findings from the SDT analysis reflect the controversy regarding the use of the stop sign at grade crossing. The general belief regarding implementation of the stop sign at grade crossings was that its message would be easily understood and could promote safe behavior. However, several observational studies have reported low rates of compliance (Burnham, 1994; Sanders, McGee, and Yoo, 1978). Similarly, in our analysis, the estimate of $\beta$ for the stop sign was generally higher than that for other warning devices, reflecting an inclination to proceed. The median estimate of $\beta$ for the stop sign in the 21-year period was 0.27, and it ranged from a high of 8.23 in 1986 to 0.04 in 2006.

Another concern is that a driver stopped at the crossing may not be able to effectively judge the speed and distance of an approaching train because visual cues regarding the lateral movement of the train are not as available. The estimates for sensitivity (ability to detect the train) may provide some evidence in this regard. The signal-to-noise ratio calculated for the stop sign were generally lower than that for other passive warning devices that encourage drivers to only slow on the approach to the crossing (e.g., the crossbuck), suggesting that the train may not be as easily detectable. Unfortunately, the signal detection analysis cannot speak to the root cause of the decisions drivers make at stop-sign protected crossings.

We also applied SDT to examine the effect of different countermeasures implemented during the time period examined. We focused on five safety factors, selected because of previous work by Horton, et al. (2008) and also discussed in Raslear (1996). We did not expect ability to detect a train or willingness to stop to change independently, but rather that an improvement in one would contribute to improving the other. The data generally showed statistically reliable improvements in d' and β attributable to both the warning device type and the introduction of the safety factor. In fact, the analysis indicated that warning devices have the most impact on grade crossing safety outcomes. A comparison of $\omega^2$ values for d' and ln β associated with safety factors and device type highlighted that the safety benefits provided by warning devices are due to their ability to encourage drivers to stop at grade crossings. Regulations to improve CMV driver safety, the use of alerting lights, sight lines, and reflectors were generally equally effective in improving safety. Warning device reliability (which pertained to active warning devices only) still contributed to improvements, but the effects were more muted.

Our data showed greater contributions for each of the safety factors examined than that reported by Horton, et al. (2008). However, our approaches to analysis and the timeframe we considered in our analyses differed. Horton, et al. calculated the percent reduction by determining the percent change in the number of incidents attributable to the safety countermeasure for the 10-year period from 1994 to 2003 (i.e., the change in the number of incidents for a safety factor from 1994 to 2003 divided by the total number of grade crossing incidents from 1994 to 2003). Rather than use accident frequency as Horton, et al. had done, our SDT model estimated metrics describing driver sensitivity and bias, which were derived using a Poisson distribution of the accident rate, and examined data for a 21-year period from 1986 to 2007. The Poisson distribution (as we applied it here) is often used to model accident frequencies because accidents are rare events and so are better described using Poisson probabilities than accident rate alone. In other words, analysis of the accident rate may not be a good way to assess safety or determine the significance of the change in accident rate.

We compared the empirical findings from our model to the theoretical predictions of the SDT model for an ideal observer who represents *optimal* decisionmaking. In general, the ideal observer analysis showed similar trends to that for each of the safety factors in the empirical analysis, although the predicted benefits for the ideal observer were somewhat greater. As hypothesized in Raslear (1996) and demonstrated in our current analysis, the combined effects of alerting lights, reflectors, train horn, and clearing of sight lines improved driver sensitivity and encouraged drivers to stop. Regulations to improve CMV driver safety, which require CMV drivers to stop at all grade crossings, were expected to be most effective at encouraging drivers to stop, but the rules also increased sensitivity by "forcing" visual search at the grade crossing in both directions of the track when the driver stopped.

The findings for the ideal observer indicate that the current signal detection model provides insight into driver decisionmaking at grade crossings. Collectively, the SDT model shows that the decision to stop (changing β) offers a greater contribution to grade crossing safety than the driver's ability to detect the train. In fact, the analysis suggests that measures that improve train detection are effective to the extent that they also encourage drivers to stop.

We believe that the SDT model described here provides a framework that can be used to understand the impact of other countermeasures for improving grade crossing safety and is more descriptive than that offered by more "traditional" analyses (e.g., accident analyses). One of the key aspects of the framework is the consideration of accident frequency with respect to human behavioral metrics that influence driver decisionmaking. In fact, the analysis shown here suggests that the examination of accident frequency alone is misleading and may minimize the impact of other important safety factors. Although the basic signal detection model is descriptive in nature, it can be refined in conjunction with field studies or laboratory experiments to provide a better understanding of driver behavior.

The findings from this analysis offer several recommendations for improving grade crossing safety. In particular, the results suggest that the greatest benefits may be obtained for those countermeasures that encourage drivers to stop at the crossing. We observed success from two such methods— legislation and education. In first considering the impact of legislation, the results from the empirical analysis showed that regulations requiring CMV drivers to stop at all grade crossings did in fact lead to increased stops; our estimates of $\beta$ improved by 70 times from 0.562 in 1986 to 0.008 in 2007. The ideal observer analysis highlighted the "value" of complying with regulations with costs (in terms of lost wages) for suspensions resulting from violations. In considering the impact of education, the results of the ideal observer analysis point to the benefits offered by education programs, which increase the "value" drivers associate with stopping for a train at a grade crossing. For example, every dollar invested in Operation Lifesaver since its inception in 1988 resulted in an equal dollar increase in the perceived value of the signal, $V(s)$. Combining education with enforcement was estimated to increase $V(s)$ by 34 percent, which reduced $\beta$ further. The results therefore suggest that further funding for education and enforcement programs can have a positive impact on improving grade crossing safety.

While the ideal observer highlighted the impact of changing $\beta$, it is important to keep in mind that countermeasures that improve d' are also effective because they indirectly help to change $\beta$. Thus, the incorporation of alerting lights and reflectors (both required by legislation) and clearing sight lines in conjunction with the use of a train horn were successful in increasing the detectability of the train at the crossing *and* encouraging drivers to stop (possibly a direct result of the increased train visibility). Therefore, other countermeasures that help to increase the detectability of the train may offer the same benefits to $\beta$.

More specifically, the SDT model and the research results described in this report point to research needs in the following areas:

1. Evaluation of different approaches to educating drivers. The framework described here points to the positive impact of public education on improving grade crossing safety—in particular, the effectiveness of the Operation Lifesaver program. However, the implementation strategies of education programs differ so that they can be tailored to community needs, but also due to variations in funding levels and resources. New media and social networking technologies have changed how information is transmitted and may allow a program to have a greater reach.

2. Evaluation of the effectiveness of highway intersection-related traffic control devices at grade crossings. In particular, data is needed to predict and understand the potential effect of yield signs— which are less expensive to install than traditional grade crossing active warning devices—at passive grade crossings and traffic signals. As part of this research, it is necessary to develop a better understanding of why stop signs have not been effective at highway rail grade crossings.

3. Definition of the circumstances in which drivers are most likely to violate grade crossings. The SDT framework highlighted the fact that the impact of active warning devices was greatest in terms of how it influenced drivers' decision to stop. Thus, a classification analysis would help identify the factors that influence driver decision at grade crossings; this in turn could lead to the development of countermeasures that address these issues (e.g., through targeted education and enforcement programs). Application of other decisionmaking theories may also be useful in predicting driver behavior at grade crossings (e.g., prospect theory) by providing insight into how the model and payoff matrix may be refined for a range of risk-taking behavior.

4. Examination of the use of traffic calming techniques with respect to the SDT framework. Traffic calming improves safety by creating stronger or weaker affordances in the environment to modify human behavior—that is, changing $\beta$. For example, rumble strips could alert drivers to the presence of the grade crossing by their sound, and also force drivers to slow down on the approach to the grade

crossing; such environmental modifications may therefore force drivers to look for the train at a grade crossing (increasing d') and encourage drivers to stop (decreasing β). However, rumble strips may also have the potentially negative effect of diverting the driver's attention away from the grade crossing to navigate the roadway.

# 7. References

Burnham, A (1994). Stop sign effectiveness at railroad grade crossings (abuse without excuse). In *Proceedings, 3rd international symposium on railroad-highway grade crossing research and safety* (pp. 91–113). Knoxville, TN: University of Tennessee.

Carroll, A.A. and Warren, J.D. (2002). Photo Enforcement at Highway–Rail Grade Crossings inthe United States: July 2000–July 2001, *Transportation Research Record, 1801,* 46–53.

Carroll, A.A., Multer, J., and Markos, S.H. (1995). *Use of Auxiliary External Alerting Devices to Improve Locomotive Conspicuity.* Cambridge, MA: U.S. DOT/FRA.

Church, R. M., and Meck, W. H. (1984). The numerical attribute of stimuli. In H. C. Roitblat, T. G. Bever, and H. S. Terrace (Eds.). *Animal cognition.* Hillsdale, N.J.: Erlbaum.

*Commercial Driver Disqualification Provision*; 49 CFR Parts 383 and 384; Final rule; published: 09/02/99; Effective Date: 10/04/99; [FHWA Docket No. FHWA-97-3103]; 64 FR 48104.

Creelman, C. D. (1962). Human discrimination of auditory duration. *Journal of the Acoustical Society of America, 34,* 582–593.

Egan, J. P. (1975). *Signal detection theory and ROC analysis.* New York: Academic.

Federal Highway Administration. Highway Statistics Series. Washington, DC: U.S. Department of Transportation, Federal Highway Administration. http://www.fhwa.dot.gov/policyinformation/statistics.cfm

Federal Railroad Administration. *Railroad Safety Statistics Annual Reports.* Washington, DC: U.S. Department of Transportation, Federal Highway Administration. http://safetydata.fra.dot.gov/OfficeofSafety/publicsite/Publications.aspx

Fitzpatrick, K, Bartoskewitz, R. T., and Carlson, P.J. (1997). *Demonstration of Automated Enforcement Systems at Selected Grade Crossings in Texas* (TX-98/2987-2F). Austin, TX: Texas Department of Transportation.

Gibbon, J. (1977). Scalar expectancy theory and Weber's law in animal timing. *Psychological Review, 84,* 279–325.

Green, D. M., and Swets, J. A. (1966). *Signal detection theory and psychophysics.* New York: Wiley.

Grier, J. B. (1971). Nonparametric indexes for sensitivity and bias: Computing formulas. *Psychological Bulletin, 75,* 424–429.

Horton, S., Carroll, A., Chaudhary, M., Ngamdung, T., Mozenter, J., and Skinner, D. (2008). *Success Factors in the Reduction of Highway-Rail Grade Crossing Incidents from 1994 to 2003.* (Report No. DOT/FRA/ORD – 09/05). Washington, DC: U.S. Department of Transportation. http://www.fra.dot.gov/eLib/details/L01592.

*Hours of Service of Drivers*; 49 CFR Parts 385 and 395; Final Rule. Federal Register 73: 224 (19 November 2008) p. 69, 567–69, 586.

Kaiser, M. K., and Mowafy, L. (1993). Optical specification of time-to-passage: Observers' sensitivity to global tau. *Journal of Experimental Psychology: Human Perception and Performance, 19,* 1028–1040.

Luce, R. D. (1986). *Response times: Their role in inferring elementary mental organization.* Oxford: Clarendon Press.

MacMillan, N. A., and Creelman, C. D. (2005). *Detection theory: A user's guide (2nd Edition)*. Mahwah, N.J.: Erlbaum.

Multer, J., Conti, J., and Sheridan, T. (2001). *Recognition of Rail Car Retroreflective Patterns for Improving Nighttime Conspicuity* (DOT/FRA/ORD-00/07). Washington, DC: U.S. Department of Transportation, Federal Railroad Administration. http://www.fra.dot.gov/eLib/Details/L04203.

Office of the Inspector General (2004). *2004 Audit of the Highway-Rail Grade Crossing Safety Program* (Report Number: MH-2004-065). Washington, DC: Federal Railroad Administration. Office of the Inspector General.

Ogden, B. D. (2007). *Railroad-Highway Grade Crossing Handbook – Revised Second Edition 2007*. Washington, DC: U.S. Department of Transportation, Federal Highway Administration.

Illinois Commerce Commission. (2005). *Public Education and Enforcement Research Study (PEERS) Phase 1 and Phase 2 (Cooperative Agreement DTFR53-03-H-00019) Final Report*. Springfield, IL: Illinois Commerce Commission.

*Railroad Locomotive Safety Standards: Clarifying Amendments; Headlights and Auxiliary Lights; Final Rule*. Federal Register 69: 51 (16 March 2004) p. 12,531.

Raslear, T. G. (1996). Driver behavior at rail-highway grade crossings: A signal detection theory analysis. In A. A. Carroll and J. L. Helser (Eds.), *Safety of highway-railroad grade crossings. Research needs workshop. Volume II – Appendices* (Report No. DOT/FRA/ORD-95/14.2, DOT-VNTSC-FRA-95-12.2, pp. F9-F56). Washington, DC: U.S. Department of Transportation. http://www.fra.dot.gov/eLib/Details/L04204.

Raslear, T. G., Akyel, Y., Bates, F., Belt, M., and Lu, S.-T. (1993). Temporal bisection in rats: The effects of high-peak-power pulsed microwave irradiation. *Bioelectromagetics, 14*, 459–478.

Reflectorization of Rail Freight Rolling Stock; Final Rule. *Federal Register* 70: 1 (3 January 2005) p. 144.

Rice, S. and McCarley, J.S. (2011). Effects of response bias and judgment framing on operator use of an automated aid in a target detection task. *Journal of Experimental Psychology: Applied, 17*(4), 320–331.

Rusak, B., and Zucker, I. (1979). Neural regulation of circadian rhythms. *Physiological Review, 59*, 449–526.

Sanders, H.J., McGee, H.W., and Yoo, C.S. (1978). *Safety Features of Stop Signs at Rail-Highway Grade Crossings* (FHWA-RD-78-40). Federal Highway Administration: Washington, DC.

Sternberg, S. (1966). High-speed scanning in human memory. *Science, 153*, 652–654.

Swets, J. A. (1996). *Signal detection theory and ROC analysis in psychology and diagnostics: Collected papers*. Mahwah, N.J.: Erlbaum.

# APPENDIX A.    SDT Analysis – Unadjusted Data

Table A-1 shows the median trains per day and AADT, calculated using data from FRA's Highway-Rail Crossing Inventory for 1986 and 2007. The highlighted cells indicate warning devices with *decreasing* levels of exposure over the 21-year period. Table A-2 presents the 2007 adjusted estimates for trains per day and AADT that were used for the current analysis. For most of the warning devices, the adjusted estimates calculated as a function of the increase in the number of trains or vehicle miles traveled (VMT) were almost twice that reported in FRA's Highway-Rail Crossing Inventory.

| Warning Device | 1986 | | 2007 Unadjusted | |
|---|---|---|---|---|
| | Trains per day | AADT | Trains per day | AADT |
| No Signs or Signals | 1.5 | 125 | 2 | 259 |
| Other Signs or Signals | 1.5 | 375 | 2 | 410 |
| Crossbucks | 4 | 125 | 2 | 110 |
| Stop Signs | 4 | 125 | 4 | 170 |
| Special Active Warning Devices | 1.5 | 3000 | 2 | 1130.5 |
| Highway Traffic Signals, Wigwags, Bells, or Other Activated Warning Devices | 4 | 750 | 4 | 767 |
| Flashing Lights | 4 | 3000 | 4 | 1530 |
| Gates | 13 | 3000 | 15 | 1473 |

**Table A-1.  Trains Per Day and AADT Values for 1986 and 2007 (as recorded in FRA's Highway-Rail Crossing Inventory)**

| Warning Device | 2007 Adjusted Estimates | |
|---|---|---|
| | Trains per day | AADT |
| No Signs or Signals | 3.28 | 213.68 |
| Other Signs or Signals | 3.28 | 641.04 |
| Crossbucks | 8.74 | 213.68 |
| Stop Signs | 8.74 | 213.68 |
| Special Active Warning Devices | 3.28 | 5128.33 |
| Highway Traffic Signals, Wigwags, Bells, or Other Activated Warning Devices | 8.74 | 1282.08 |
| Flashing Lights | 8.74 | 5128.33 |
| Gates | 28.42 | 5128.33 |

**Table A-2.  2007 Adjusted Estimates for Trains Per Day and AADT (based on number of trains and VMT, respectively)**

The values for d' and beta, calculated using the *un*adjusted estimates of trains per day and AADT, are provided in Table A-3. A comparison of the estimates for d' using the raw exposure data with that for the adjusted data (in Table 2) shows little difference; in fact, the overall mean d' was the same regardless of the method used to estimate exposure. Examination of the individual d' values for each warning device shows that the adjusted estimates for $\lambda_T$ and $\lambda_H$ led to a slight decrease (on the order of 0.02 and 0.07 points) in the estimated d' for six of the eight warning devices. The two warning devices that showed an increase in d' as a result of the adjustment were the special active warning devices, which increased by 0.12 points, and flashing lights, which increased by 0.04 points.

A comparison of the estimates for β using the unadjusted and adjusted trains per day and AADT estimates shows a more striking difference. The mean β dropped from 0.34 with the unadjusted exposure rates to 0.02 with the adjusted rates. Additionally, the pattern of results shown by the unadjusted data is somewhat questionable. First, the data suggests that drivers were more likely to proceed than stop at crossbuck-protected crossings, with a β estimate of 1.68. This value is higher than that calculated in 1986 (0.67 as shown in Table 3), despite data showing that accidents had dropped at crossbuck-only crossings in the 21-year period (from 2,224 in 1986 to 569 in 2007). Second, a comparison of the β values for the different passive warning devices indicated that drivers exhibited the riskiest behavior at crossbuck-only crossings, but the results of field studies and accident analyses suggest that use of the stop sign at grade crossings actually results in more noncompliance than the use of crossbucks alone. Thus, the interpretation of the findings for β as shown in Table A-3 was inconsistent with other data and research results, so we sought alternative ways to estimate exposure and improve our SDT model of driver decisionmaking.

| Warning Device | 2007 | |
|---|---|---|
| | d' | Beta |
| No Signs or Signals | 7.56 | 0.1270 |
| Other Signs or Signals | -- | -- |
| Crossbucks | 7.29 | 1.6752 |
| Stop Signs | 7.05 | 0.4826 |
| Special Active Warning Devices | 7.29 | 0.0317 |
| Highway Traffic Signals, Wigwags, Bells, or Other Activated Warning Devices | 7.13 | 0.0259 |
| Flashing Lights | 7.13 | 0.0093 |
| Gates | 6.94 | 0.0010 |
| AVERAGE | 7.20 | 0.34 |

Table A-3. d' and Beta Values for 2007 (as calculated using the unadjusted values for trains per day and AADT)

# APPENDIX B.   Accidents per Safety Factor

The number of accidents attributable to each safety factor in 1986 and in 2007 is shown in Table B-4.
Two numbers are provided: one that shows the total number of accidents attributable to that safety factor
(i.e., includes accidents with multiple safety factors), and the other that provides the isolated number of
accidents attributable to *only* that safety factor.

### (a) CMV Driver Safety

| Warning Device | 1986 | | 2007 | |
|---|---|---|---|---|
| | Total | Isolated | Total | Isolated |
| No Signs or Signals | 25 | 16 | 4 | 4 |
| Other Signs or Signals | 11 | 3 | 0 | 0 |
| Crossbucks | 730 | 463 | 154 | 131 |
| Stop Signs | 96 | 59 | 68 | 56 |
| Special Active Warning Devices | 34 | 19 | 4 | 3 |
| Highway Traffic Signals, Wigwags, Bells, or Other Activated Warning Devices | 74 | 49 | 4 | 3 |
| Flashing Lights | 494 | 308 | 92 | 68 |
| Gates | 239 | 132 | 184 | 135 |

### (b) Alerting Lights

| Warning Device | 1986 | | 2007 | |
|---|---|---|---|---|
| | Total | Isolated | Total | Isolated |
| No Signs or Signals | 26 | 17 | 3 | 3 |
| Other Signs or Signals | 13 | 6 | 0 | 0 |
| Crossbucks | 582 | 418 | 88 | 69 |
| Stop Signs | 80 | 55 | 41 | 30 |
| Special Active Warning Devices | 35 | 25 | 4 | 4 |
| Highway Traffic Signals, Wigwags, Bells, or Other Activated Warning Devices | 53 | 37 | 5 | 4 |
| Flashing Lights | 472 | 347 | 80 | 66 |
| Gates | 456 | 363 | 322 | 268 |

**Table B-4.  Accidents Associated with Each Safety Factor:  (a) CMV Driver Safety Regulations,
(b) Alerting Lights, (c) Reflectors, (d) Increasing Sight Lines, (e) Warning Device Reliability**

| (c) Reflectors | | | | |
|---|---|---|---|---|
| **Warning Device** | **1986** | | **2007** | |
| | Total | Isolated | Total | Isolated |
| No Signs or Signals | 3 | 2 | 0 | 0 |
| Other Signs or Signals | 3 | 1 | 0 | 0 |
| Crossbucks | 271 | 187 | 44 | 37 |
| Stop Signs | 33 | 21 | 11 | 11 |
| Special Active Warning Devices | 30 | 20 | 6 | 5 |
| Highway Traffic Signals, Wigwags, Bells, or Other Activated Warning Devices | 26 | 21 | 4 | 4 |
| Flashing Lights | 229 | 180 | 49 | 42 |
| Gates | 108 | 86 | 82 | 78 |

| (d) Increasing Sight Lines | | | | |
|---|---|---|---|---|
| **Warning Device** | **1986** | | **2007** | |
| | Total | Isolated | Total | Isolated |
| No Signs or Signals | 5 | 2 | 0 | 0 |
| Other Signs or Signals | 2 | 0 | 0 | 0 |
| Crossbucks | 199 | 89 | 24 | 17 |
| Stop Signs | 23 | 9 | 3 | 2 |
| Special Active Warning Devices | 8 | 0 | 2 | 1 |
| Highway Traffic Signals, Wigwags, Bells, or Other Activated Warning Devices | 18 | 8 | 0 | 0 |
| Flashing Lights | 88 | 45 | 15 | 7 |
| Gates | 37 | 14 | 12 | 6 |

| (e) Warning Device Reliability | | | | | | |
|---|---|---|---|---|---|---|
| **Warning Device** | **1986** | | **1997** | | **2007** | |
| | Total | Isolated | Total | Isolated | Total | Isolated |
| No Signs or Signals | -- | -- | -- | -- | -- | -- |
| Other Signs or Signals | -- | -- | -- | -- | -- | -- |
| Crossbucks | -- | -- | -- | -- | -- | -- |
| Stop Signs | -- | -- | -- | -- | -- | -- |
| Special Active Warning Devices | 0 | 0 | 0 | 0 | 0 | 0 |
| Highway Traffic Signals, Wigwags, Bells, or Other Activated Warning Devices | 2 | 2 | 9 | 4 | 2 | 1 |
| Flashing Lights | 11 | 4 | 88 | 44 | 15 | 8 |
| Gates | 13 | 6 | 96 | 40 | 37 | 23 |

**Table B-5. (continued). Accidents Associated with Each Safety Factor: (a) CMV Driver Safety Regulations, (b) Alerting Lights, (c) Reflectors, (d) Increasing Sight Lines, (e) Warning Device Reliability**